FULL
CIRCLE

A History of the City of Edinburgh
Universities' Officers Training Corps

George O. Sutherland

Lynne Reilly for
Edinburgh Universities' Joint Military Education Committee

Published in 2014 by Lynne Reilly on behalf of
Edinburgh Universities' Joint Military Education Committee
University of Edinburgh
Old College
South Bridge
Edinburgh
EH8 9YL

ISBN: 978-0-9931392-0-8

Publication layout and design by Lynne Reilly
(lynnereillypublishing@gmail.com)
Front cover images: Annual Camp 1923 (Edinburgh University
Library, Special Collections and Archives, Acc. 1999/017)
and CEUOTC cap-badge (OCdt Eve Stott).
Back cover image: Remembrance Day Parade, Old College
Quadrangle, November 2014 (OCdt Luke Craggs).

Printed and distributed by:
Witley Press Ltd
24–26 Greevegate
Hunstanton
Norfolk
PE36 6AD

Contents

    Pipes and Drums
    Victoria Cross Winners
    Uniform Notes
    The University Infantry Volunteers
    The University Medical Volunteers
    The University Artillery Volunteers
    Timeline
    Officers Commanding the OTC Units
    Commanding Officers
    Second-in-Commands
    Training Officers/Training Majors
    Adjutants
    Unit Camps
    Contingent Camps
    Trophies

HRH The Duke of Edinburgh. Prince Philip was appointed Royal Honorary Colonel of the City of Edinburgh Universities' Officers Training Corps in 2004, having been Honorary Colonel since 1953.
© Crown Office

I am delighted that this story of what is now the Edinburgh Contingent of the Officers Training Corps has been written. The unit has a long and distinguished history. As long ago as 1859, staff and students at Edinburgh University trained as riflemen, gunners and medical staff in University Volunteer Units. In 1908 they combined to form one of the very first University OTCs in the country.

Most valuable to the nation in times of war, or the threat of war, these volunteer units provide basic military experience for young people during the final stages of their academic education. Learning military discipline, acquiring basic military skills and experiencing the demands of command, all contribute to the vital process of becoming a valuable member of society.

The Corps as a whole, and The City of Edinburgh Universities' Officers Training Corps in particular, have always aimed high and can be justifiably proud of their record.

Acknowledgements

MANY PEOPLE ASSISTED in the preparation of this history in a variety of ways and I am grateful to them all. Inevitably, some were able to contribute significantly more than others and I trust they will understand it is not possible for me to make any equitable distinction. They and I know who they are. If anyone has been omitted, that is an error on my part for which I apologise.

At the University of Edinburgh, the Principal and Vice-Chancellor Professor Sir Timothy O'Shea, Deputy University Archivist Grant Buttars and his staff, Secretary to the Joint Military Education Committee Susan McGinley, at the Graduates Association Peter Freshwater and John Sutherland, Jen Middleton, Press and PR Officer. Bryden Ritchie, Convener, and the members of the JMEC also provided invaluable encouragement, support and tangible help.

At City of Edinburgh UOTC, the Honorary Colonel Sir Malcolm Rifkind, Lt Col Gordon Mackenzie, A/Lt Col Major Miles Hutchinson, Major Neil Potter, Major Eddie Walsh, Captain Torquil Corkerton and Captain David Freeman; former Commanding Officers David Bayne, James Collins, Ron Abbott, Ian Hamilton, Stuart Crawford, Ewart Baxter, James Hancock and Doug Mackay; former Training Majors Alastair Cumming and Adrian Williams; former Adjutants Tom Buchanan, Charles Inness, Derek Lawson and Julie Murray; Officer Cadets Olivia Atkinson and Eve Stott. Former SSgt Forrest Anderson helped in several ways and has an extensive archive of material to which he allowed me generous access. I sincerely hope that they, perhaps having a special interest, find the finished product to their liking.

Help was also provided in specific areas by General Sir Mike Jackson, Major General Stuart Skeates Commandant RMA Sandhurst. Daren Bowyer of the Sandhurst Trust, Brigadier John Thomson, Colonel Allan Lapsley, Professor Sir Hew Strachan, Professor Gary Sheffield, John Cameron and Ian Davidson of the Western Front Association, Sarah Dalman, librarian at the National War Museum of Scotland and Patrick Anderson.

As a class of contributor, however, it is the former cadets and Officer Cadets who perhaps did most to give 'flavour' to this record: Vivian Abrahams, Jim Allan, Mike Blair, Andrew Campbell, Jim Fraser, James Fairbairn, Alasdair Geater, Sheena Gillespie (nee McKelvie), Bill Gillespie, Don Grocott, Stuart Irvine, Julia Kneale, Fred Lawson, Diarmid Lindsay, Scott Lindsay, George Livingstone-Learmonth, Kenneth MacDonald, Iain Maclaren, Fiona Maclaren (nee Heptonstall), Nigel Malcolm-Smith, Alexander McCall Smith, Hamish McLaren, Shaun Murphy, Hamish Nicholson, John Poynton, Douglas Proudlock, Stephen Rae, Scott Robertson, Richard Scott, Ronnie Seiler, Bill Simpson, Hamish Smith, Douglas Walker and John Woodman.

Enormous thanks are due to Lynne Reilly for designing and editing the end product.

Finally, I owe a debt of gratitude to my wife Jackie, not only for her assistance and patience over the last ten months, but also for her wisdom in encouraging me to undertake the project in the first place.

Preface

IN DECEMBER 2013, I was approached by the Commanding Officer, Lt Col Gordon Mackenzie with an invitation. Edinburgh OTC was one of the original eight OTCs formed in 1908, but it was also one of very few whose history had never been recorded; would I be willing to address this unfortunate omission?

I suspect that he and Bryden Ritchie, my successor as Convener of the Edinburgh Military Education Committee (MEC), felt that as I was retired, had some limited experience as a TA officer, had served on the MEC for almost 20 years and was interested in military history generally, I might be a willing candidate.

I was, not realising that there were virtually no records other than the skimpy and incomplete formal minutes of the MEC from 1908, MEC Annual reports to Senate (not accessible after 1949) and Minutes of COMEC, recording issues affecting the Corps nationally. There was also a well-researched manuscript prepared by Lt Col Alistair Harwell (CO 2000–02) covering the period 1859 to 1908 in detail plus a brief overview up to 1919. Initially, the proposal was that I would cover the period 1919 to date, but it seemed to me necessary to start at the beginning of the OTC at least, namely 1908. As research progressed, it became clear that there was not sufficient information to produce any sort of detailed Unit history but there was enough to cover its ever-changing role and, crucially, the national background and environment in which it operated. At least to some extent, this would set it apart from other OTC histories and compensate for the lack of parochial information and perhaps result in a publishable document. If that were to be the case, it would make sense to start at the very beginning,

1859, and incorporate Alistair Harwell's work, at least in summary form.

The project had taken shape and the final product is intended to be a readable account of the origins, achievements and principal events in the history of City of Edinburgh Universities' Officers Training Corps.

For reasons given above there has been no attempt to list day-by-day, or even year-by-year activities, as that would be unreadable. For example, the text generally does not mention annual camps individually unless there is some significance or a special event to report but the reader will find the locations of camps listed in an appendix.

The same principle applies to Commanding Officers, Second-in Command, Training Officers/Training Majors and Adjutants, who are also listed in appendices as far as has been possible.

Equally, I have not attempted to compile statistical data such as the number of cadets gaining Certificate A or B, or, later, passing MTQ1 or MTQ2, or being commissioned into the Regular or Territorial/Reserve Forces. The available records simply do not contain sufficient information but it is clear that the Unit has an excellent record in all of these measures and throughout its history has compared favourably with other University Contingents. A fortunate exception is the numbers commissioned in WWI.

Similarly, the appendix on uniforms contains as much information as it has been possible to ascertain, but I am conscious of the many gaps. Many hours were spent trying to find answers but increasingly this became unproductive and I had to settle for 'Notes'.

The biggest, and to my mind most unfortunate omission, is the lack of information on Warrant Officers and NCOs. It would have been appropriate and highly desirable to list the RSMs along with the COs and other key staff members but the available records name them only rarely.

Similarly, and equally regretted, there is only passing reference to the Permanent Staff Instructors. In one sense, they are the backbone of the OTC and the men with whom the cadets have most contact. Their selection and performance is crucial and it is to the great credit of the Army and the individuals themselves that many former cadets, who can be hard to please, speak highly and warmly about their former instructors.

I have also endeavoured to incorporate personal accounts and anecdotal material wherever possible. It was interesting, and at times very frustrating, to discover that those who were cadets in the 1940s, 50s, 60s and even 70s were very supportive and forthcoming, making contributions and encouraging friends to do likewise. The chapter on the 1963 exercise in Norway illustrates the value of this. By contrast, there is virtually no anecdotal material from the last two decades despite many contacts; it might be that cadets in those years are too busy with careers or family responsibilities to contribute or perhaps they assumed that I would have ample material from such recent times.

Finally, here is an example of a great deal of background work that produced no results. The term 'Officer Cadet' was introduced at RMA Sandhurst in 1939 and in the OTC in 1958 although it had occasionally been used informally before that, referring to cadets generally as 'officer cadets'. Before 1958, OTC cadets had standard army ranks, but the photograph of the 1931 Bisley champions gives the rank of one cadet as 'O. Cdt'. Neither the National Army Museum, the Scottish National War Museum, the National War Museum Library, The Imperial War Museum nor the librarian or archivist at Sandhurst could offer an explanation; it is a national mystery!

This book does not purport to have all the answers, but it does contain as much of the Unit's meaningful history as I have been able to gather.

G. O. Sutherland
Edinburgh
November 2014

Chapter 1

Forerunners[1]

NO SCOTTISH MILITARY unit has a longer history of unbroken volunteer service than that of the City of Edinburgh Universities Officers Training Corps (OTC).

Although the OTC as such was formed in 1908 as part of a wide-ranging restructuring of the British Army led by Richard Haldane, Secretary of State for War and an alumnus of Edinburgh University, the Edinburgh Contingent can trace its origins to 1859.

At that time, the Army was recovering from the casualties suffered in the Crimean War, which had ended only three years previously and had cost the lives of over 21,000 British soldiers, mostly through disease. The following year, the Indian Mutiny had required addressing, and in 1859 many battalions were still deployed there dealing with the aftermath, leaving a seriously depleted army to defend the British Isles.

Meanwhile, France had expanded its army to be the largest in Europe and was indulging in an alarming level of sabre-rattling and threatening behaviour towards Britain and others. The nation was anxious, with the people of London taking to the streets to demand that more be done to defend the country. The War Office (WO) was forced to act.

On 12th May, the WO wrote to all Lord-Lieutenants inviting them to co-ordinate the formation of Volunteer Rifle Companies (VRC) and Edinburgh's students responded immediately. Despite a warning that Volunteers would be unpaid and would need to provide their own weapons, ammunition, uniforms and equipment, a group of undergraduates met at 6 York Place on 14th May and resolved to form a VRC. They approached the University authorities and ten days later Professor Robert Christison (a leading academic and the Physician to Queen Victoria in Scotland) called a general meeting of staff and students in the chemistry classroom at what is now known as Old College. The room was crowded, with over 500 in attendance (according to *The Scotsman*) and the decision was taken to form a University Rifle Company.

The University was not alone: within weeks the Lord Provost (as Lord-Lieutenant of Edinburgh) had applications to form nine Companies and called a meeting at Edinburgh City Chambers of representatives of all the VRCs in Edinburgh. Here it was decided to form a Regiment: the City of Edinburgh Rifle Volunteer Corps (CERVC) of which the University Unit would be No. 4 Company under the command of Captain Allen Dalzell. Dalzell worked in the Chemistry department and had served for seven years as a sub-altern in the 27th of Foot. (Although it seems clear that Edinburgh University was the first body to decide to form a VRC, seniority was allocated on the basis of the order in which the Lord Provost had received formal applications.[2])

Not surprisingly, the expense of providing weapons and equipment had restricted the number of volunteers and a decision by the WO in December to issue Enfield rifles led to a surge in recruitment. By August 1860, CERVC had 20 Companies, divided into two Battalions, and No. 4 (University) Company had 90 riflemen. In Scotland as a whole, there were over 20,000 Volunteers and on 7th August a Royal Review of Volunteers took place in Holyrood Park. 1st Battalion CERVC, including No. 4 Company, led a parade of 21,514 men as it marched past Queen Victoria in front of 200,000 spectators.

Later that month, Captain Dalzell resigned and was replaced a few months later by Professor Christison.

As the threat of a French invasion subsided, so did the volunteers' enthusiasm and numbers began to dwindle across the nation. In response, the Government passed the Volunteer Act of 1863. Henceforth, VRCs would receive an annual grant of £1 for each 'efficient' volunteer plus a 10/- bonus (50p) for each volunteer who had fired at least 60 rounds and was qualified as a 2nd Class Shot.

(To be efficient a volunteer had to attend at least six battalion and three company drills in the year. Recruits had to attend thirty drills including musketry and obtain a certificate of competence.)

In 1866, the Edinburgh Corps was granted a major honour: Regimental orders proclaimed that,

> 'Her Majesty has been graciously pleased to approve of the 1st City of Edinburgh Rifle Volunteer Corps bearing the designation of THE QUEEN'S CITY OF EDINBURGH RIFLE VOLUNTEER BRIGADE'. (QERVB)

Establishment was fixed by the WO at 2,500 in 25 Companies of 100 each, the largest in Britain, and the Brigade adopted the practice of providing recruits with their uniform and all equipment, excluding boots, free of charge on the strict understanding that they made themselves efficient. On the other hand, COs were now empowered to impose fines such as £1 for becoming inefficient. This had the desired effect; whereas in the early 1860s the proportion of efficients was typically 30–40% it quickly rose to 80–90% and by the late 1870s 95–100% was the norm in most Companies in the Brigade. However, this demand was perhaps at the expense of recruitment and retention, and No. 4 Company was one of the few that generally maintained a full complement.

Following the defeat of the French by the Prussians at the Battle of Sedan on 1st September 1870, Britain reassessed its military preparedness. In 1871, power over the Volunteers was transferred from Lord-Lieutenants to the Secretary of State for War and all volunteer riflemen were issued with Snider Enfield breech-loading rifles. The renewed interest in VRCs boosted recruitment with a further 49 undergraduates enrolling in No. 4 Company, taking the Unit's strength over its authorised establishment. This was permitted probably because other Companies in the Edinburgh Brigade were typically under-strength.

In 1872, Captain Sir Robert Christison, completed his 50th year as a professor of Edinburgh University. To mark the occasion 83 members of No. 4 Company, under the command of Lt Turner, paraded on 23rd February. They formed three sides of a square at the west end of the quadrangle in Old College and presented arms as a Guard of Honour escorted Sir Robert from his classroom to his position in front of the Company.

Lt Turner made a gracious speech, referring to Christison's role in making No. 4 Company one of the *'largest and most efficient'* in QERVB and adding *'as individual members we would venture an expression of the high regard we entertain towards you personally, and of our esteem for your character as a man of honour and a true gentleman'*.

Christison replied eloquently and at considerable length, addressing his comments to *'Lt Turner, Ensign Robertson and Gentlemen of the University Company ...'*, expressing his gratitude and pride. The entire speech is quoted in the *The Queen's Edinburgh Rifle Volunteers (QERV)* (p. 188) but one section has particular relevance in the context of this history:

> *The position of a captain of volunteers – and particularly a captain of volunteers of the University – is peculiar, and it is one which in many respects is a most agreeable one. In the first place, he is commanding officer and is entitled in that particular to your obedience. This I have always received. But besides, many of you are his own students, and you are all students of the University – men who in a short time will be on a level with your officers and who are therefore entitled to be treated from the first as in great measure upon the level ...*

He then went on to describe the level of skills and knowledge an officer required over and above those needed by a private soldier and the clear inference is that even then the University volunteers were automatically regarded as potential officers. Although there was no syllabus of special officer training the Company aspired to standards higher than their nominal role required. The deliberations of Senate and the Military Committee in considering an application by H Company of the 9th Battalion, The Royal Scots, for recognition as a University formation, provides further evidence of this ethos of preparing all volunteers to officer standard if not knowledge (see page 12).

QERV also contains a description of the sword presented to Sir Robert:

> [It is] *a very handsome one, richly chased and ornamented. On the hilt there is a bugle with a crown above the bugle knot. The blade, on which are engraved the motto of the city, Sir Robert's own motto, 'Vitam dirigat', and various emblems, bears the following inscription: 'Presented to Sir Robert Christison, Bart, Captain of No. 4 University Company, and senior Captain of QERVB, by the members of the Company, as a mark of their esteem and appreciation of his energy, courtesy and enthusiasm in promoting its welfare, 23rd February, 1872'.*

Another significant event in 1872 was the completion and occupation by Edinburgh's Rifle Volunteers of a new, purpose-built Drill Hall at Forrest Hill, not far from Old College. The University Company was to be based there for 36 years and the same building was later the home of Edinburgh OTC for an identical period, from 1957 to 1993.

Over the next decade a number of significant events occurred. In July 1877, Christison retired and was replaced by Captain William Turner who had been a member of the Company since its formation in 1859 and had served as Christison's deputy for 17 years. He was Professor of Anatomy and would go on to become Principal and Vice-Chancellor of the University. Two years later, QERVB held its first annual camp, on Lanark Moor, and around this time was issued with Martini-Henry rifles. The following year, No. 4 Company won the inaugural Scottish Inter-University Shooting Competition.

On 25th August 1881, the second Royal Review of Volunteers took place at Holyrood Park. Almost 40,000 Volunteers, including 1,573 from QERVB, paraded for long hours in atrocious weather in what was to be known ever after as 'the Wet Review'. Sadly, some reporters estimated that over 200 men died as a result of the ordeal.

In April 1884, the University Company paraded to provide a Guard of Honour between Parliament House and St Giles' Cathedral on the occasion of the Tercentenary of the University of Edinburgh. The celebrations included a grand banquet in the Volunteer Hall at Forrest Hill.

This year also saw the formation of the University medical volunteers.

Despite the inadequacies of medical care in the Crimean War, which had resulted in more men dying from disease than enemy action, volunteer units still had little formal medical support. Most battalions had a medical officer but there was no provision for stretcher-bearers or field hospitals. This omission was widely recognised and in many units enlightened officers and NCO instructors gave informal training in first aid and stretcher work but more was required. Surgeon-Major George Evatt, a medical officer at the Royal Military Academy Woolwich, and a London surgeon, Dr James Cantlie, had been lobbying the WO for more formal provision within the volunteers and toured the country to spread the word and gain support for their cause.

In November 1884, they visited Edinburgh and met with the Lord Provost and the senior army Medical Officer in Scotland. They then met J. H. A. MacDonald, Colonel of QEVRC, who had initial concerns that the formation of a medical unit would potentially draw men away from one of his best rifle companies, No. 4, which was manned in large part by medical students, but agreed to call a meeting of the students. Evatt addressed an audience of around 150 medical men with such eloquence and enthusiasm that they determined there and then to form an informal company of medical volunteers. The elected commandant was Dr Charles W. Cathcart, an assistant surgeon at the Royal Infirmary, who had been the senior student in No. 4 Company in 1878. Although they received no financial support and had no uniforms, the medical volunteers trained diligently in the work of a field ambulance.

In April 1885 the WO approved the formation of the Volunteer Medical Staff Corps and early the following year recognised the University medical volunteers as the Edinburgh Company, 2nd Division, Volunteer Medical Staff Corps (VMSC), with Cathcart gazetted as Surgeon in command. Training comprised mainly route-marching and camping, for instance in the Trossachs and on several occasions at Kinross House. From 1891, annual camps were at Aldershot where all the VMSC units joined the army's autumn manoeuvres; with 25,000 participants, accidents were inevitable and the medical staff gained experience in handling real casualties. The Unit did not train with the Rifle Volunteers and there seems to have been no interaction socially.

In 1888 the QERVB was re-designated the Queen's Rifle Volunteer Brigade (QRVB), The Royal Scots, affiliated to The Royal Scots (Lothian Regiment). It was split into three battalions with the University Company being the senior in the 3rd Battalion but, at its own insistence, retaining its designation as No. 4 Company.

In January 1890, Captain Sir William Turner resigned as Company Commander but continued to show a keen interest in the Company. In choosing his replacement, the University had regard for academic standing rather than military skills or experience and appointed Isaac Balfour (Professor of Botany), who had been a member of the Company for less than two years.

Around this time, the University Battery was formed.

In 1860 the 1st Edinburgh City Artillery Volunteers (ECAV) had been established as Garrison Artillery to man fixed guns defending vital positions such as the harbours along the south side of the Forth estuary. By October it had nine Batteries although it had difficulty in keeping them fully manned.

In 1889, 1st ECAV was allocated eight 16-pounder field guns and was directed by the WO to form two Position Batteries to support the Forth Volunteer Infantry Brigade. These Batteries would deploy with the infantry to give direct fire-support, that is engaging targets the gunners could see, as had been the practice ever since artillery first appeared on the battlefield. These mobile guns with their horse teams and ammunition limbers required larger crews than the fixed guns and ECAV sought to address this problem by amalgamating four garrison Batteries into two Position Batteries, numbered 1 and 2 while the remaining Garrison Artillery Batteries were renumbered 3 to 7.

This arrangement did not fully resolve the manpower issue and, as the gun-teams in mobile artillery had to be fully manned in order to function properly, it was necessary to recruit more men. However, this was not readily achievable in a city where there were already sufficient volunteer units to absorb those with the desire to serve. Perhaps aware that Aberdeen and St Andrews Universities had gunner units, ECAV turned to University of Edinburgh. While the exact sequence of events has not been established, it is clear that by 1891, No. 2 Battery ECAV was manned by undergraduates and staff of the University and recognised as a University Unit.

This was birth of the Battery that was to play a major role in the life of the University and frequently parade, and be paraded, with considerable pride.

It is interesting to note that for decades, the annual University Calendar described the Battery as having been founded in 1859. Apart from the minor discrepancy in the year, the inference that it had been a University Unit since then is clearly incorrect. However, in asserting that it was 'the oldest Artillery OTC in the kingdom', the *History of the University of Edinburgh 1883–1933* (Logan Turner, 1933) is correct. Both Bangor and St Andrews Universities had Batteries in 1908 but they did not transfer to the OTC. Cambridge OTC is described as having an Artillery Unit when it was formed[3] but this is misleading; it had permission to form such a Unit, and promptly did so, but did not receive guns until January 1909.

The University Rifle Company was now facing stiff competition in recruitment, and to increase its attractiveness, the Company requested one of the new Maxim machine-guns recently introduced into the Regular Army. This was delivered in February 1893 and is believed to have been the first machine-gun in Scotland.

The celebrations to mark Queen Victoria's Diamond Jubilee were held in London on 22nd June 1897. QRVB cancelled Annual camp and paid for three men from each of its Companies to attend. Others, including eight from the University Battery and a group from the Volunteer Medical Staff Corp paid their own way and a total of almost 200 Edinburgh Volunteers sailed from Leith on 19th June on board S.S. *Malvina* arriving at Tower Bridge early on Monday morning. On Tuesday, the contingent fell-in at 8 am and marched behind pipers to their rendezvous at Horse Guards Parade and on to their position at the western end of the Mall. The day was gruelling, standing stiffly at attention in the heat and the Edinburgh men were grateful that they were on the shaded side. After the procession they marched straight back to the ship and sailed for home.

The required standards of training for the Rifle Volunteers had become more stringent, particularly in marksmanship, and No. 4 Company's enthusiastic new commander, Captain Hope, sought to exceed these. In the absence of a Brigade Camp he organised a week-long 'marching column' in East Lothian. On the 23rd July, the Company paraded at Old College and marched to Waverley Station where they entrained for Longniddry, from where they marched the eleven miles to North Berwick. After resting on Sunday, they marched over the rest of the week via Dunbar, Gifford and Haddington back to Old College.

Meanwhile, the Battery was effectively being run by the second-in-command, Lt Hobson. Instead of participating in the annual Scottish Artillery Association competition at Barry, he took the Battery to the National Artillery Association competition at Lydd.

In December, the Company was re-equipped with Lee Metford rifles which fired the new cordite-propelled .303 bullet with a much higher velocity, and hence range, than the Martini-Henry. This meant that the Hunter's Bog range was now unsafe, as high shots could reach built-up areas of the city. Fortunately, this was readily remedied by re-aligning the range to fire west to east with Arthur's Seat as a backstop.

The Volunteer Units played an increasingly prominent role in the life of the University and in 1898 No. 4 Company was allocated two places on the Students' Representative Council and all three units paraded at the opening ceremony of the McEwan Hall.

In October 1899, the Boer War started and several early and embarrassing reversals demonstrated that the Army would need reinforcing. The University Company volunteered its Maxim machine-gun with one officer and 38 riflemen but this offer could not be taken up as the conditions of service of the Volunteer Companies precluded overseas service. This did not prevent individuals enlisting privately and several members of the Company went to South Africa with the 1st Volunteer Service Company, Royal Scots.

The Medical Company also volunteered for active service. It was not required as a unit but the WO invited the members to apply for one-year attachment to the Regular Army Medical Staff Corps and around 40 did so. Those who did not deploy spent annual camp at the Cambridge Military Hospital in Aldershot (1900) and at the Royal Victoria Hospital in Netley (1901). Here, hospital ships arrived almost daily bringing casualties from the front. Of the 21,000 British soldiers who died as a result of the campaign, over 16,000 did so from disease, leading to a hasty review of the medical services and a major re-organisation. The 2nd Division VMSC became the Edinburgh Company RAMC (Volunteers).

The war also affected Volunteer Rifle Companies. Establishment was increased to 116 all-ranks and there was a surge in recruitment with the total number of Scottish Volunteers rising in the first twelve months of the war from 49,322 to 57,485. No. 4 Company continued to be stronger than its authorised establishment and in 1900/01 had 177 efficient members. Training and uniform were also modified as a result of lessons learned. The grey uniform was replaced by brown 'drab' and a slouch hat was introduced while training concentrated on fire-and-movement rather than frontal assault which had proved so costly and futile against Boer positions.

In 1902, the Battery also experienced change. 1st ECAV became 1st Edinburgh (City) Royal Garrison Artillery (Volunteers). Simultaneously, Position Batteries were re-named as Heavy Batteries and the University unit became Left Half, 1st Heavy Battery, 1st ECR-GAV.[4] Despite the change in title, the Battery was still equipped with the antiquated 16-pounder muzzle-loaders and enthusiasm was beginning to wane. By the end of the year, manpower had fallen to less than 70 effective members, but things were about to change dramatically.

In January 1903, the Battery was re-equipped with 4.7 inch QF [Quick Firing] guns which could fire a 45 lb shell with considerable accuracy up to a distance of 6,000 yards.

This allowed the men to learn the new skill of 'indirect fire', namely shooting at targets the gun-crews could not see, guided by instructions from an Observation Officer in a forward position within sight of the target. In the summer the Battery, now commanded by Captain F. P. Dods, won the Artillery Championship of Scotland and repeated the feat in 1904 and 1905. In that year they were also runners-up in the Heavy Artillery Championship of Great Britain.

On 18th September 1905, all three University Units took part in the third and final Royal Review of Scottish Volunteers at Holyrood Park when 38,383 volunteers paraded before King Edward VII.

At a meeting of the University Senate on 13th January 1906, a letter from Lt Col James Clark was read, requesting that Senate recognise H Company, 9th Volunteer Battalion (Highlanders) Royal Scots, as a University Company. After debate, it was initially proposed to refer the matter to the Principal and Deans Committee for consideration, but a counter-proposal to approve the request was carried.

This provoked a swift reaction from the existing University Units and the following was presented to Senate at its next meeting on 3rd February 1906:

To the Senatus of the University of Edinburgh
Petition by
No. 4 (University) Coy, QRVB, RS,
No. 2 (University) Batt. ECRGA (V)
and
The Edinburgh Company RAMC (V)

Your Petitioners have heard with very great concern that, at a recent meeting of the Senatus, official recognition was promised to H Company, 9th VB (Highlanders) RS as a University Corps.
The Petitioners hoped that, before any such action was taken, their opinions and views would be asked, as the question

is one which vitally affects their interests, so vitally that they have felt constrained to present this Petition, and humbly request reconsideration of the question.

It may be pointed out that the War Office never sanctions the formation of a new Corps without first consulting with the Regiments holding the same field.

Senate remitted the Petition to the Principal and Deans Committee, instructing them *'to hear parties, including Captain Huie, on behalf of H Company, and to report'*.

At its meeting on 3rd March, Senate received a report from the Principal and Deans Committee dated 26th February. They had met with representatives of No. 4 and H Companies at which Captain Huie argued that as his Company appealed especially to high-landers it was a *'different constituency'*. Nevertheless, No 4 Company felt that, if H Company were raised to full establishment from its current strength of 60 (including six pipers and drummers who were not students), its own numbers could be seriously reduced from the present 135 and seriously interfere with its *'role as a training school for commissions in the army'*. This is explicit confirmation of the University Volunteers' self-appointed purpose; they were not merely predecessors of the OTC but were a model for it, a fact not lost on Lord Haldane. It was noted that a total of around 700 students were serving in the various Volunteer Units in Edinburgh.

Again there was debate and a resolution to rescind the recognition of H Company was moved and seconded. However, an amendment was moved and also seconded seeking to confirm the earlier recognition and the matter was put to a vote. The amendment was carried, but with the caveat *'provided the Military Committee is satisfied with the willingness and ability of H Company to furnish adequate training for candidates for Commissions in the Army'*.

On 1st June, the Military Committee reported to Senate that it was not satisfied that the Company could afford adequate training. The Senate Minutes do not record any further discussion or decision but, as there is no subsequent university record of H Company as a University Unit, it seems clear that the judgement of the Military Committee, as was to be expected, concluded the matter. Curiously however, H Company is again mentioned in the context of the OTC in Army Orders in 1908 and no doubt it was this reference that led to it being described in *The Queen's Edinburgh Rifle Volunteers* as having become part of Edinburgh OTC. This is clearly incorrect, as explained below.

In the summer of 1906, the Battery was beaten in the Scottish competition at Barry but was again runner-up in the national championship at Lydd. The following year, Captain R. G. Gordon assumed command and in August, the Battery won the Heavy Artillery Championship of Great Britain, receiving the coveted King's Cup. The following day, *The Scotsman* reported '*no praise can be too high for the excellence of their practice*' and this is no exaggeration. Competing against every Volunteer Battery in the kingdom, the young students had consistently performed better than opponents with much more experienced gun crews and observation officers and had finally achieved the ultimate prize. It was a superb achievement!

Around this time, there was the first hint of the OTC. The Battery Diary records that, at the Battery's annual dinner held in Ferguson & Forresters with a large number of distinguished academic and military guests, Professor Hudson Beare, chairman of the Military Committee (later the Military Education Committee – MEC) proposed the toast to the Imperial Forces in the course of which he outlined '*the new scheme for the Officers' Training Corps as far as was possible at that time*'. The Battery Secretary's annual report went on: '*but unfortunately Col Powles who replied, apparently thought it his duty as a "Regular" to sniff at the attempt to create amateur officers of artillery*'.

On the morning of 10th January 1907, the Right Hon. R. B. Haldane, KC, MP, Secretary of State for War and Lord Rector of University of Edinburgh, delivered his Rectorial Address in the McEwan Hall and afterwards inspected the three University Companies in the quadrangle of Old College.

In 1908, the Haldane Reforms came into effect on 1st April, establishing the new Territorial Force (later to become the Territorial Army) and the Officers Training Corps.[5] Special Army Order Number 72 of 16th March 1908 covered the formation of the latter and invited Universities and Schools to host Contingents of the Senior and Junior Divisions respectively.

This was followed two days later by another Special Army Order listing the Volunteer Battalions and Companies that would transfer to the Territorial Force and highlighting those which would not do so immediately, pending the possible creation of OTC Contingents by their host institutions.

The latter listed the Units attached to universities, Edinburgh being the only University with more than one: No. 4 Company, the Battery, the Medical Company and H Company! The only other artillery Units were No. 3 Company, 1st Carnaervon RGA at University College Bangor and No. 7 Company, Fifeshire RGA at St Andrews; neither made an early transfer to the OTC.

Although the Edinburgh Medical Company went to annual camp in 1908 as OTC, the first tranche of eight OTC Contingents was officially recognised as having been formed on 1st September 1908 as specified in Army Order 297 issued on 10th November 1908. These were Birmingham, Cambridge, Durham, Manchester, Oxford and Wales, each with Infantry Units, Belfast (newly-formed) and Edinburgh with Infantry, Artillery and Medical Units. The Infantry comprised No. 4 Company; H Company did not become part of the OTC.

No. 4 Company marked the occasion by parading from the Forrest Hill Drill Hall, down Chambers Street past the Old College, to the OTC's new accommodation at High School Yards in Infirmary Street.

Chapter 2

The First Decade

THE BOER WAR had demonstrated that the Regular Army was too small to undertake prolonged major campaigns and the country required a significantly larger force that would be available to support the Regulars in time of national emergency. At it simplest, this was the role of the new Territorial Force.

The role of the OTC was primarily to prepare undergraduates for commissioned service and to maintain a supply of well-educated officers to the Territorial Force. No one could have foreseen how vital this was to become.

It was required that a host university had a Military Education Committee (MEC – the usual but not universal title) comprising a mix of university and service representatives to oversee the operation of the OTC with particular regard to the balance between cadets' military and academic activities. The University of Edinburgh, in common with most academic institutions that had Volunteer Companies or Batteries, already had a Military Committee for that very purpose and it merely had to adopt the new title.

The University of Edinburgh's was one of eight original OTC Contingents, but more would soon follow.

Contingents' officers became Territorial Force officers and were generally members of the University staff, although non-staff of similar standing, such as medical staff at the Royal Infirmary or Chartered Accountants, lawyers and the like were also be appointed. Each Contingent had a Regular Army Adjutant as Staff Officer, responsible for administration and the programme of lectures and instruction, supported by Regular NCO instructors.

Cadets were referred to as such but had normal army ranks such as Private or Gunner and could be promoted to Corporal, Bombardier, Sergeant, and so on. They received no pay and had to contribute an annual membership fee towards the running of the Unit, but uniforms and all equipment were supplied.

The cadets' training was geared towards them obtaining Certificates A and B, although many of those who had served in the Junior Division at school would already have the former. Certificate B was relatively demanding involving practical tests and three written papers on 'Requirements of an Officer', 'Military Law' and 'King's Regulations', plus a further technical paper for Royal Artillery candidates. The examinations were voluntary but brought benefits; Certificate B together with a Unit commander's recommendation qualified the cadet for a Territorial Force commission.

There was no Commanding Officer and the Infantry, Artillery and Medical Units trained separately and held their annual camps at different locations and times allocated by the WO. Any overlap was coincidental and there was no social interchange; the Units were more likely to relate to their counterpart Units from other Universities. However, all the Officers Commanding and the Adjutant were members of the MEC so there was coordination of the use of training facilities, both at High School Yards and Weekend Training Camps.

Each year, there were two training camps, one in Spring over the Victoria Day weekend and a two-week summer camp. In each of the next four years, the Battery attended annual camp at Barry or Buddon, between Monifieth and Carnoustie (now known as Barry-Buddon), while the Medical Unit went to Aldershot. The Infantry generally avoided going to the same location in successive years; their first camp as OTC was at Stobs, a few miles south of Hawick in the Scottish Borders, then Barry, Blair Atholl and back to Stobs in 1911. After the war, this variety would become the norm for all except the Battery, who were restricted to artillery firing ranges, although they did have some choice e.g. Barry, Redesdale in Northumberland and occasionally Larkhill, the School of Artillery near Salisbury.

The Battery did not have a chance to defend its national title.

The National Artillery Association decided that, as it was not part of the Territorial Force, it was ineligible to compete, but in other respects the OTC status brought several benefits. In 1909, the Infantry were authorised by the WO to raise a third Company and to form a *'Pipes and Drums Band'*, which would *'adopt kilts and pipe ribbons of the McFarlane tartan'*.[6]

In a letter dated 7th January 1910, the WO sanctioned the raising of an Engineering Unit and in a further letter, dated 11th January 1910 (in response to a request from the MEC), advised that the Artillery Unit was to be converted from a Heavy Battery to a 6-Gun Battery equipped with modern 18-pounder field guns. As the new guns would not be delivered from Woolwich for several months, the RFA Regiment based at Piershill in Glasgow loaned two 18-pounders to enable conversion training of the cadets to begin immediately. A request to raise a Unit of mounted infantry was declined.

On 28th October around 300 cadets paraded in Old College quadrangle under the command of the Adjutant, Captain Clive. They were inspected by the Lord Rector of the University who praised their role in addressing *'one of the weakest links in the chain of our defences ... the provision of trained and capable officers to fill up places in case of emergency'*.

The following year, 45 EOTC cadets were part of a 500-strong OTC Battalion that lined the streets of London during the King George V's Coronation and State Procession through the city on 22nd and 23rd June respectively and the following month a large proportion of the Contingent paraded in Windsor Park when the King reviewed the OTC.

Around this time the Medical Unit attracted the attention of the authorities in more ways than one. In May the WO had written to the University expressing satisfaction at the progress of the Unit and authorising the raising of a second section of Field Ambulance. At Annual camp in Aldershot, however, a number of cadets were reported by the Military Police as having created a disturbance. An MP Sergeant wrote:

> *I saw a large number of NCOs and men of the OTC in Welling-ton Street. They were marching along six abreast, arm-in-arm, and behaving in a very disorderly manner. I afterwards assisted the Civil Police to eject several of them from the George Hotel public bar.*

The police tried to arrest two of them but, assisted by their friends, they escaped and were last seen sprinting towards the camp. The WO wrote to the University asking that the culprits be identified and expelled from the Corps as *'they were unfit to wear the King's uniform'*. The University, perhaps hoping that the issue would not be pursued, replied that it could do nothing until after the summer vacation.

Lt Gen H. L. Smith-Dorrien, GOC-in-C, Aldershot Command then wrote to his counterpart in Scottish Command saying that he considered the matter of such importance that he had brought it to the attention of the Army Council. The University had to act; an investigation was initiated and three cadets *'confessed that they had misconducted themselves'*. Taking into account their otherwise good behaviour both in the OTC and in their studies, they were instructed to resign from the OTC. All three were later commissioned and served in the RAMC in WWI.

This sequence of events makes clear that the OTC held the attention of the highest echelons of the army.

In November 1911, Captain J. R. Bruce, commanding the Infantry Unit, applied to the MEC for permission to adopt the kilt, feeling this would greatly enhance recruitment. A special committee was appointed to report on the subject and in 1912 approved the proposal. The Earl of Seafield, head of the Clan Grant, gave his consent for the Infantry Unit to wear Clan Grant tartan (which was Black Watch tartan or very similar[7]) and the new uniforms were introduced in 1913.

There was an issue over inter-unit relationships. The Medical Unit always trained and socialised separately and this seems to have been generally accepted, but the new Adjutant, Captain J. C. W. Connel KOSB, was not content to accept the distance the Infantry kept between themselves and the Battery and Engineer Units. The latter two had developed a happy rapport, perhaps because they saw themselves as sharing a need for more technical skills. Connel, however, being a professional Regular officer, understood the need for close co-operation between all arms and set about arranging inter-unit visits and exercises to foster the level of mutual understanding that he knew to be necessary on the modern battlefield.

Annual camp in 1913 was a Brigade Camp at Ilkley with over 2,000 Infantry cadets from all over Britain. The Edinburgh, Glasgow and St Andrews contingents formed No. 3 Battalion of which Captain J. R. Bruce, OC the Edinburgh Infantry Unit was Second-in-Command.[8] Over the Victoria Day weekend in 1914, the Infantry undertook a route march in Angus, finishing at Barry where the Battery, the Engineers and the St Andrews Contingent were already encamped and were astonished to be invited by the Battery to a 'smoker' in the evening with them and the Engineers. (A smoker was a popular Victorian pastime, a men only social event, sometimes with musical entertainment, where the issues of the day were discussed.) Perhaps Captain Connel's efforts were paying dividends.

In the summer, the Engineers camped at Carlingnose Point at North Queensferry and constructed rope bridges over a ravine, while the other Units went to Stobs.

Then everything changed. On 3rd August 1914, Belgium refused free passage for the German Army intent on invading France and was itself invaded. Britain gave an ultimatum to withdraw by midnight or face the consequences. There was no withdrawal and the following day Britain declared war on Germany.

Immediately, the Adjutant and Regular instructors returned to their regiments and all the heavy equipment, notably the artillery guns, was withdrawn. In addition, several of the officers and many of the cadets immediately volunteered for the front line and left. From the Infantry Unit, the OC, Captain J. R. Bruce and all eleven subalterns went to the front. Bruce was posted missing presumed killed at La Boiselle on the first day of the Battle of the Somme[9] and six of the seven subalterns who joined the infantry died on the Western Front.

Between 4th August and 31st December, 442 cadets and former cadets were commissioned, 167 into the infantry, 150 Royal Artillery, 79 RAMC and 49 Royal Engineers.[10] The numbers were soon replenished as a new intake of undergraduates proved keen to undergo military training alongside their academic studies. Total strength of cadets in the Unit on 30th September 1913 was 451 and on 31st December 1914 it was 564.[11]

In October, Major J. E. Mackenzie, commanding the Artillery Unit, was appointed acting Adjutant.

After August 1914, the training for Regular officers continued to be at Woolwich for the Royal Artillery and Royal Engineers, and Sandhurst for other Arms but the duration of the courses was reduced to three and six months respectively. By 1917 this had been extended to eight and twelve months.[12]

The rapid expansion of the Territorial Force (Kitchener's so-called New Armies) created an immediate demand for many more 'temporary' officers, but there was no prearranged plan for their training. In the first month of the war, most received a one-month course at an OTC, but the numbers being commissioned and the urgency with which they were required were so great that this could not be continued and for the remainder of 1914 new officers were sent to their battalion directly upon being commissioned. This was expedient in the short-term but was clearly unsatisfactory, and, early in 1915, Schools of Instruction were established at OTCs to provide four-week courses for such men. The WO approached The University of Edinburgh to enquire whether it would be willing to *'organise and run a School of Instruction for young officers in connection with the OTC'*. This was approved by senate and delegated to the MEC *'with powers'*.[13]

An Infantry School was established immediately and its first course commenced on 22nd April with 52 young officers attending and Major Mackenzie and Lt Gentles of the Infantry Unit among the instructors. At Major Mackenzie's suggestion, an Artillery School was also established and its first course began on 25th May.

During 1915, three courses were held at each of the two Schools attended by 208 Infantry and 73 Artillery officers. A further, Infantry course was held early in 1916, with 74 officers attending but this was to be the last, as the Army got its act together and the system changed.[14]

In the meantime, the OTC had moved to full-time training for undergraduates and others who intended to enlist but continued part-time training for medical students and others who wished to continue their studies.[15] This level of activity in addition to the School courses placed enormous demands on all the staff. The Battery Diary noted *'all the senior officers of the OTC are preoccupied with the Schools of Instruction'*, leaving the junior officers and NCOs to conduct the undergraduate OTC training. To allow all this to happen, the University relieved those officers on its staff of their academic responsibilities.

On 25th January 1916, under the command of the Adjutant, 250 cadets and 30 junior infantry officers (who were in Edinburgh to attend the course at the School of Instruction commencing the following day) gave a demonstration of gun drill, physical training and stretcher work at High School Yards to the Lord Provost, Sir Robert K. Inches. They then marched up to the quadrangle at Old College where they were inspected by the Lord Provost and the Principal, Sir William Turner (who was to die suddenly a few weeks later).[16] On 9th February, General E. C. Bethune, Director-General of the Territorial Force, inspected a further parade of 345 cadets.[17]

The rapid training of young officers had been unavoidable in the early stages of the war when Kitchener's 'New Armies' were being formed but it had always been recognised that the hasty training provided nothing more than very basic rudiments. By the autumn of 1915 there had actually been a glut of newly, but inadequately, trained 2nd Lieutenants and a revised training programme was introduced from February 1916. Until that date, cadets had been commissioned directly from the OTC into their regiments where they received the necessary further training. This had several drawbacks, not least the burden on the regimental officers themselves. From 1916, cadets would be trained in OTCs until reaching the age of 18½ when they would transfer to an Officer Cadet Battalion (OCB). Twenty-seven OCBs were established including two at each of Cambridge and Oxford and two in Scotland at Gailes in Ayrshire. Each had an establishment of 400 cadets and the course lasted four months.

The Schools of Instruction such as those run at Edinburgh were no longer required. New Schools, run by the Regular Army, were established to provide a higher level of instruction for young officers who had originally received only limited training but now had several months experience with a regiment.

As military service became compulsory in 1916, the role of the OTC diminished and it provided little more than a few months basic training to school leavers before they enlisted – whether to an OCB or not. Training continued to be full-time for those intending to enlist, but 'non-intensive' for others such as medical students who were to complete their studies. Cadet numbers continued to be between 300 and 400 and the Battery Diary noted that the average time a cadet served in the Battery was 18 months.

The Battery was partially re-equipped receiving two of the latest model of 18-pounder QF guns in 1916 to supplement two elderly 15-pounder BLC guns that had arrived the previous year.

On 10th December, the Principal, Sir James A. Ewing inspected the Unit at High School Yards and addressed the 228 Cadets on parade, noting that

> 'the OTC can rightly and properly claim to have conferred a very great benefit on the country. In 1914, the Edinburgh OTC immediately supplied 500 officers from its own ranks, followed by many hundreds' in the two years since'.[18]

By 1917, the training of officers was well-organised with a ready supply of experienced officers and NCOs who were recovering from wounds and not fit for the front, but who were well capable of carrying out training and instruction roles. Against this background, the OTC continued its more traditional role of providing part-time instruction for undergraduates while continuing full-time training for those intending to enlist but not old enough to enter an OCB. This continued until the end of the war.

The training and discipline were rigorous. A University student who was called up and entered the OTC at this time was Alastair Sim, later to become famous as an actor in many popular films. His biographer noted:

He loathed the OTC with its oppressive and rigid discipline ... his strong reaction against the dehumanising stricture of army life helped him to develop his own beliefs in the right of the individual to freedom and self-expression.

On 11th November 1918, to mark the armistice, the Battery and the Engineer Units formed up in Old College quadrangle and paraded via North Bridge, Princes Street, the Mound and George IV Bridge to New College (the Medical School) and back to Old College.

Ten days later, the King and Queen, together with the Prince of Wales paid a Royal Visit to Edinburgh. After a service of thanksgiving for victory at St Giles' Cathedral, they proceeded to the Usher Hall. Here the King was presented with a civic address in a gold casket and '*His Majesty, in reply, paid a splendid tribute to Scotland for the part she had played in bringing the war to a successful conclusion*'. Their Majesties then continued to South Bridge, lined by 300 cadets of Edinburgh OTC, and Old College where the Principal, Sir Alfred Ewing, wearing his black and gold robe over a khaki uniform, presented a Loyal Address.[19]

Immediately after the end of the war, a new adjutant, Captain C. Preston DSO, was appointed and Major John Mackenzie turned to compiling *The Edinburgh University Roll of Honour 1914–19*, published in 1921.

It lists 944 alumni who had made the ultimate sacrifice and also give details of decorations awarded to university staff, graduates and undergraduates who had served. These include 5 Victoria Crosses (two of which were to former OTC cadets), 175 Distinguished Service Orders, 705 Military Crosses, 5 Distinguished Service Crosses (Royal Navy) and 6 Distinguished Flying Crosses (RAF, formed 1st April 1918).

There is no record of the awards to former cadets, other than a note in the Battery Diary which states that the total decorations awarded to former members of the Battery were '*approximately nine DSOs, sixty MCs, one Croix de Guerre and one Ordre de Merite plus an unknown number of MiDs*'. These figures are almost certainly understated due to annual entries being treated as cumulative when a simple analysis suggests they were not.

Captain Preston also undertook research and published two informative tables in the War Memorial edition of *The Student* published in 1921.

NUMBER OF CADETS TRAINED DURING WWI AT EDINBURGH OTC

YEAR	ARTILLARY	ENGINEERS	INFANTRY	MEDICAL	TOTAL
1914/15	298	95	383	209	985
1915/16	310	19	167	238	734
1916/17	366	10	158	170	704
1917/18	392	76	157	169	794
TOTAL	1,366	200	865	786	3,217

OFFICERS COMMISSIONED FROM EDINBURGH OTC

UNIT	1908 to 4th August 1914	August 1914 to November 1918	TOTAL
ARTILLARY	41	803	843
ENGINEERS	6	135	141
INFANTRY	44	756	800
MEDICAL	43	557	600
TOTAL	134	2,250	2,384

Chapter 3

The Inter-war Years

EARLY IN 1919, the Battery Diary records that training had reverted to five hours per week instead of full-time, '*but there is little attendance*'. This was not restricted to the Artillery Unit, or to Edinburgh, it was the same throughout the country.

The WO wrote to the University on 20th March 1919:

The [Army] Council feel, with the inevitable reaction after the cessation of hostilities, that the Officers' Training Corps movement may languish. They do not, therefore, wish at this moment to bring pressure to bear on members of the University who are possibly war-weary, but they consider that the remainder of the present academic year should not be allowed to pass without steps being taken to prepare for the future. With this end in view they ask that preparations be made to select officers and leaders who will come forward in October next to raise interest and enlist sympathy among members of the University. In fact, the foundations should now be laid, on which it will be possible to restore the contingent to at least its pre-war numbers and efficiency.

The WO was not alone in looking to the future. Within OTCs there had been widespread dissatisfaction at several aspects of the mobilisation, notably the treatment of OTC officers and cadets who enlisted for active service. Officers were treated as substantive 2nd Lieutenants regardless of their Territorial Force rank and cadets arriving at an Officer Cadet Battalion were treated as fresh recruits even if they held Certificate B.

The past and present officers of London OTC had prepared and circulated to MECs a report dated 15th October 1919 and titled 'Future of the OTC'. This was based on the lessons learned in the war and the intention was to agree a set of proposals to be presented to the Secretary of State for War aimed at improving the organisation of the OTCs, rationalising the status of Cadets and being better prepared for any future mobilisation.

The London proposals were:

1) *The Senior Division of the OTC should become a distinct Corps entitled 'OTC'.*

2) *The Junior Division* [in schools] *should be separate and have its own name and organisation.*

3) *On the outbreak of war necessitating the mobilisation of the Territorial Force, the OTC should be similarly embodied, expanded and adapted to train officers for the 'augmented establishments' and to replace casualties.*

    a) *In peacetime, the War Office should pay grants to Universities to cover the costs of officers and Cadets.*

    b) *Provision should be made in the OTC for specialised military works, particularly those involving the application of science to war.*

    c) *There should be a scheme whereby the War Office can give selected soldiers from the ranks of the Regular Army the opportunity to study at University and train in the OTC with a view to qualifying for commissions in the Regular Army.*

The Edinburgh MEC adopted the proposals and '*desired that, if approved by Senate, they be transmitted to the Secretary of State for War*'. The letter was sent.

Field Marshall Sir Douglas Haig had been awarded an Honorary Degree in the McEwan Hall on 28th May 1919. As he travelled from Holyrood Palace via Canongate, South Bridge, Chambers

Street and Forrest Road to the McEwan Hall, escorted by The Royal Scots Greys, the streets were lined with cheering onlookers. Upon arrival he inspected a Guard of Honour of the OTC.

The only other event of note in 1919 was the arrival of a generous allocation of Lee Enfield rifles and Lewis light machine-guns for the Infantry Unit.

The WO responded to the OTC proposals in a letter dated 7th July 1920:

1) *The Senior and Junior Divisions of the Officers Training Corps must remain as such, inasmuch as both were originally formed in 1908 for the same purpose.*

2) *The Army council are opposed to handicapping Universities in their academic instruction by embodying a University Contingent in this way on the outbreak of war.*

On the question of finances, the letter stated that, since the Capitation Grant had recently been doubled, any further review would be deferred.

The Central Organisation of Military Education Committees (COMEC) discussed the response at a meeting in London on 16th October and a sub-committee was appointed to propose a position for discussion with WO representatives.

On 18th March 1921, the COMEC sub-committee met with members of the General staff and made the following points:

1) *Many OTCs were in financial difficulties.*

2) *COMEC still felt that it was not ideal to call both the Senior and Junior Divisions by the same name.*

3) *Status of the Senior Division in peace and war. After mobilisation in 1914, very great discontent was occasioned by these kinds of inconsistencies:*

   a) *No arrangements were made for the use of our contingents in the event of mobilisation.*

> b) *Cadets applying for commissions were treated exactly as other candidates and their training in Officer Cadet Units was largely a repetition of that in the OTC.*
>
> c) *Officers of the OTC were unpaid and the ranks they held in the Territorial Force were ignored when joining active units.*

COMEC recommended that cadets be paid the same amount as soldiers in the Territorial Force. The response from the General Staff was:

> 1) *On mobilisation OTCs would become Officer Training Units Each university was requested to present proposals as to how they would convert to OTUs on mobilisation. (If the Territorial Force were to be mobilised the War Office would have an established requirement for 10 Officer Cadet battalions.)*
>
> 2) *The matter of OTC officers being treated as substantive Second Lieutenants was being addressed.*
>
> 3) *Permanent staff such as the Adjutant and NCO Instructors would not be transferred upon mobilisation.*
>
> 4) *OTC Officers would receive payment for lecturing cadets when replacing Regular Officers.*[20]

It would be almost 20 years before the nation again mobilised, and by then these proposals were either overtaken by events or forgotten.

The Principal, Sir Alfred Ewing hosted a reception in the Playfair Library in Old College on 27th October 1921 for the OTC and first year students with the aim of boosting recruiting but the attendance of freshers was disappointing.

The Officers Commanding Units had considered the WO request for proposals on conversion to an OTU. Their plan assumed that National Service would be in force and was conditional upon the provision by the WO of more instructors, the necessary equipment and the same pay as the Territorial Force.

The specific requirements for each Unit were as follows:

Artillery (strength 150): to take over the hostel at Craigmillar Park and stabling for 80 horses and a gun park would be required.

Engineers (strength 120): to be based at King's Buildings and use Dreghorn Ranges.

Infantry: to form 2 Double Companies and combine with another university to form an Officer Cadet Battalion (OCB).

Medical: as medical students would be exempt from National service to complete their studies, they would be unpaid and no additional facilities would be required.

The MEC agreed with the plans and the Conveners of the Scottish MECs were to meet to '*secure, if possible, uniformity in the replies to the War Office letter*'. There is no record of the eventual submission to the WO, but the lack of further debate suggests that the response had sufficed.

Spring and summer camps were held annually with increasing frequency of camps being shared by Units, although the Medical Unit was more likely to be independent and the Artillery summer camp was usually at a firing range.

Over the next few years, cadet numbers steadily improved and by 1924 strength was over 300 cadets and growing. For the next 15 years it would consistently be between 350 and 400.

Alistair Campbell McLaren (MB ChB 1929) joined the OTC in 1924 and later in life recorded reminiscences:

I joined the Medical Unit of the OTC and can only say that I did so for the fun of it as I had no leanings towards military life. The Medicals had a reputation for wildness and to some extent were envied by the other sections of the OTC. The infantry wore the kilt and carried rifles! The Engineers wore breeches and puttees <u>and</u> carried rifles. The Battery wore breeches and puttees and had to cope with horses and guns. But *the Medicals had the glamour of wearing the kilt and did <u>not</u> have any rifles to lug about with them. We also had the advantage that we were <u>all</u> medical students – University and Colleges. Some medical students joined the Battery (mainly, I think, for the horses) but I never heard of any medicals in either Engineers or Infantry – fancy carting a rifle about all the time.*

I did not attend many parades during term-time and concentrated on going to the camps, one at the Victoria Day weekend and mainly the Summer Camp. Had I seen into the future, I would have tried to get my Certificates – A and B – and then when I joined the Territorials I would have gone straight in as a Captain!

He goes on to describe the 1925 Spring Camp at Montrose where he was astonished to see his contemporaries drinking significant quantities of beer in the canteen. The Saturday evening exploit was to 'capture' a large goldfish sign above the entrance to a fish shop. This was duly accomplished, but led to a visit by the police the following morning. The fish was surrendered and the matter was closed. Although nothing more was said officially, *'the good people of Montrose swore the Universities would never be allowed back!'*

Annual Camp at Shorncliffe entailed much route-marching including one particularly long route in high temperatures.

We marched very well as we had the pipe band with us – each unit had one or two pipers, and in between the pipes we sang marching songs, usually bawdy ones. We were very proud of our Commanding Officer, Dr F. A. E. Crewe who marched the whole way with us, and we were equally annoyed with the Camp Commandant who not only rode a horse the whole way but also was known to refer to us – the Infantry and the Medicals – as bare-arsed barbarians. We knew him as Swing Belly!

In 1926, a 'Contingent' dance was held and appears to have been the first occasion since the Principal's Reception in 1921 when all the Units came together for any sort of event. In November, a booklet describing the activities of the OTC was produced and distributed to many schools in Edinburgh and the surrounding district with the aim of encouraging future students to join its ranks. The booklet included introductory letters of encouragement from the Chancellor and Principal of the University and the GOC Scotland. The Prime Minister was also invited to contribute but declined as he was '*too busy dealing with the* [national] *strike difficulties*'.

The following year, a small-bore shooting club was formed and the MEC presented a trophy to be competed for annually by teams.

The 1928 Annual Camp at Scarborough was attended by the Scottish and several English Contingents who were inspected by Field Marshall Sir G. Milne GCMG KCB DSO. He declared that the Contingent's performance was '*highly satisfactory, except for discipline which must be tightened up considerably*'.

A letter sent by the Town Clerk of Scarborough to the Adjutant of Durham OTC soon after the camp, provides evidence. Headed 'DAMAGE CAUSED BY OTC', the letter was surprisingly amicable and acknowledged that the cadets' behaviour was '*due to high spirits, not malice*' and the town looked forward to welcoming them back at some future time. As a gesture of goodwill, the Town Council was prepared to '*waive the balance if the OTC sends £20*'.

Unfortunately, 'high spirits' were not unusual and at camp in Nairn the following year, the Infantry and Medical Sub-units had to pay damages. This was followed by the MEC receiving a letter from the railway company that had transported the cadets describing their behaviour on the train as '*disgraceful*' and referring to '*the throwing of articles out of the carriage windows*'. It was left to the OCs to deal with the matter but the MEC made it clear that any recurrence would be regarded as extremely serious.

In 1929, the OTC again provided a Guard of Honour for HRH Prince George at the opening of the new Zoological Building in King's Buildings on 15th May and by the end of the year, strength was over 370 Cadets with 90% efficient, which the Adjutant considered unsatisfactory but the MEC thought *'thoroughly satisfactory'*!

In 1931 the Contingent sent an Inter-unit team to Bisley where they distinguished themselves by winning the Inter-University Shooting Cup. This was reported in an article for the University Journal.[21]

> *Perhaps the greatest feather in our caps and glengarries is the work of the Shooting Team; in Scotland they won several individual prizes and gained the Inter-Universities Trophy at Bisley … . The Cup itself is a very handsome one presented last century by Mr Henry Whitehead and competed for by Volunteer Units. The Queen's Edinburgh Rifles won it for five years in succession in 1902–06, and in 1925 it was handed over by the National Rifle Association for competition in the O.T.C. Senior Division Competition.*
>
> *Once again it comes to Edinburgh.*
>
> *The Camps this year were successful in spite of bad weather and the unfortunate occurrence at Catterick where three officer cadets in the Engineer Unit were struck by lightning, and considerable damage was done to equipment.*
>
> *The Artillery Unit returned to Buddon and again received the admiration of all gunners who saw them as well as the Inspecting Officer, Colonel W. G. Lindsell, O.B.E., D.S.O., M.C.*

(It is interesting to note the term 'officer cadets', which was not in general use; even at Sandhurst, the students were 'Gentlemen Cadets' until 1939. The term probably stemmed from the 'Officer Cadet Battalions' established in 1916 to train officers as described in Chapter 2.)

The Bisley feat was repeated in 1932, EUOTC becoming the first Contingent to win it in successive years, but the following year they were beaten into second place by London OTC, by one point!

There were no annual camps in 1932 due to financial constraints occasioned by extensive reconstruction at High School Yards but they resumed in 1933. In 1934 all Units except the Artillery camped at Callander where they were inspected on 17th July by Major-General B. C. Freyberg, VC, CMG, DSO, LLD of the General Staff of the WO. He stated in his report that he had never seen a *'better turned-out OTC Contingent'*. The following year again saw all Units receiving first class reports including the following comments: *'An efficient Unit, ably commanded and well officered … . This is a Unit which takes itself very seriously, and in which there is great esprit de corps'.*

In 1936 there was a major and enduring change – the appointment of the first Commanding Officer. This had first been considered in the MEC in 1923 but it was only now that the decision had finally been taken.

Major F. J. C. Moffat DSO, Officer Commanding the Engineer Unit, was promoted to Lt Col and appointed to the post with effect from 1st July. Moffat had attended George Watson's College where he played in both the 1st XV and 1st XI. He joined the University of Edinburgh in 1913 as a medical undergraduate but on the outbreak of war had volunteered for a commission. After two months training in the OTC Artillery unit, he was commissioned into the 10th Bn Gordon Highlanders.

In 1917 he won an immediate DSO, gazetted on 22nd March 1918:

T/Captain Francis John Campbell Moffat,
Gordon Highlanders.

For conspicuous gallantry and devotion to duty in an attack. He was in command of the right attacking company, which was opposed to a very powerful system of the enemy's defences. He led his company forward with the greatest courage and determination under heavy fire, but they were eventually held up by a machine-gun firing from a concrete emplacement. This he attacked single-handed, putting all the team out of action. He was badly wounded during this encounter, but, inspiring his men to further efforts, he led them several hundred yards further before

he fell exhausted. His splendid courage and determination were
undoubtedly responsible for the success of the attack.

After the war, he resumed his sporting interests and later became
an international rugby referee, officiating at the 1932 match in
Swansea when Wales beat England 12–5.

In 1937, the Artillery Sub-unit (as the four branches were now
termed) was issued with gun-tractors and became mechanised
rather than horse-drawn and with war clouds again on the horizon,
the Unit's Establishment was increased to 520.

The CO initially felt that the new recruiting target was possible
to achieve but would be facilitated if the MEC could strive to get
the OTC *'more within the orbit of the University'*. This comment
is notable. In 25 years the OTC had changed from being a prominent, important and integral part of the University to something
more peripheral. In a hand-written note prepared at this time, Moffat observed:

Although the Corps is now an organisation of which the Uni-
versity can well be proud, it does not appear to be receiving,
from the University in general, the full measure of support to
which it is entitled in these difficult times.

In the event, recruitment in both 1937 and 1938 was disappointing
and the CO reported to the MEC that it would be impossible to
reach Establishment.

Perhaps as a consequence of Moffat's appeal to the MEC, the
Principal of the University, Professor Sir Thomas Holland, spent a
weekend with the Unit during its annual camp at Catterick and
addressed the cadets.

On 8th July 1937, HM The Queen was awarded an Honorary
Degree in the McEwan Hall. Before her arrival, the OTC paraded
at High School Yards and marched behind the Pipes & Drums to
Bristo Square. A hand-picked Guard of Honour from the Infantry
Sub-unit took their position by the entrance to the hall with the
band close by while the remainder of the cadets lined the Queen's

approach route. On both the Queen's arrival and departure, the Guard presented arms and the Pipes & Drums played a Royal Salute.[22]

In 1938, the Unit fired its first 21-gun Royal Salute from Edinburgh Castle. The following year it fired three and the custom has continued, almost uninterrupted, to the present day with the Unit firing the Salute on the Royal Honorary Colonel's birthday on the 10th June each year.

With war seeming increasingly likely, the Territorial Army was greatly expanded in 1939 and this rendered it impossible for the WO to provide instructors and material for OTC camps; they were all cancelled. However, the very continuation of OTCs, which had been in doubt, was confirmed[23] and the international situation encouraged recruitment with strength rising to 553 against the Establishment figure of 520.

Chapter 4

The Senior Training Corps

ON THE OUTBREAK of war, all heavy equipment, notably the artillery pieces, were removed for more important use elsewhere and training for all Sub-units became infantry-based. Unlike during WWI, all officer-training was to be carried out by the Regular Army at Officer Cadet Training Units (OCTUs) and the OTC was to continue its peacetime role of training undergraduates to obtain Certificate B.

At the request of the WO, the Edinburgh OTC, bolstered by two regular officers appointed for the task, opened a Reception Unit to deal with applicants for commissions during the voluntary period. During the six months of its operation, it processed approximately 3,000 applicants of whom around 1,000 went to the Army and the vast majority of the remainder to other services or essential industries. The Unit closed on 9th March 1940.

During the Spring term of 1940, the MEC made representations to Senate requesting a relaxation in the number of hours of obligatory class attendance in order to allow the members of the OTC a better chance of attaining the standards required for Certificates A and B. Senate responded immediately. It felt that the urgency of the situation demanded a response that showed the University's willingness to meet it. It was also recognised that it would be unfair to all concerned to distinguish between members of the OTC and others, so, with effect from 14th February 1940, all classes and laboratory work on Fridays were discontinued for the Faculties of Arts and Law and those Science subjects which included OTC members. Medicine, Divinity and certain technical Science branches were unaffected as undergraduates in these subjects were 'reserved', and not liable for OTC service.[24]

Senate reasoned that faculties would maintain *'standards'* but would need to reduce the *'scope'* of degree courses. This sacrifice would be compensated by the course for the WO Certificates *'which is of high educational value, and provides an admirable supplement and corrective to the purely academic work of the lecture room, the library and the laboratory'*.

Women students, and men who for whatever reason were not members of the OTC, would not enjoy this benefit, but it was felt could *'make much of it good by private study and by other kinds of service'*.

A decision from the WO was still awaited as to whether there was to be a change of role for the OTC, but intake had been restricted to those aged between 17½ and 19½ years of age. In September, the OTC was renamed the Senior Training Corps (STC) to avoid confusion with the Officer Cadet Training Units (OCTU) and in October the WO announced that the STC was to be expanded in order that all male students could enrol and would be part of the Home Guard. The OTC became the 9th City of Edinburgh (University STC) Bn, Home Guard.

At the same time, under a separate WO initiative, the University of Edinburgh was invited to run a series of special six-month science courses for potential Royal Artillery officers prior to their attending OCTU. The first course started in October 1940 with around 40 men attending and studying mathematics, physics, chemistry, and engineering as well as undertaking a limited amount of training with the STC.

Former Artillery officer Vivian Abrahams attended a later course:

> *I enlisted in the army in April 1945 and requested to be considered for the Royal Artillery University Short Course programme. On VE Day I attended a selection committee which I passed and which assigned me to the 11th Special Army Entrance Royal Artillery at the University of Edinburgh. So, that October, in company with about thirty other members of the Royal Artillery,*

I was dropped off at my digs to train for a war that had ended by having an academic year at Edinburgh University. Although we had passed WOSB and completed around six months training, we were still Gunners and during term time had to attend mandatory military training with the Senior Training Corps. I recall that we had to answer to a Col Buchanan-Smith. During vacations we were given a short leave and then moved into barracks and conducted artillery weapons training. After being commissioned and serving in Europe, the Middle East and North Africa I was demobbed in 1948. I returned to Edinburgh University as a student and embarked on a scientific academic career.

So the University Short Course turned out to be a critical career decision, but more for introducing me to Edinburgh University than for advancing my military career.

Also in October 1940, the OTC Unit of The Royal Dick Veterinary College was disbanded with the Cadets transferring to Edinburgh STC and the Artillery Sub-unit was able to resume gunnery training equipped with MkI and MkII 18-pounders.

On 22nd March 1941, the Unit provided a Guard of Honour when the President of the Polish Republic, Mr W. Raczkiewicz, formally pronounced the establishment of the Polish School of Medicine in Edinburgh.

Several significant events occurred in 1941. The Principals of the Scottish Universities decided to make it a condition of entry to university that all male students join either the STC or the University Air Squadron[25] and, in the autumn, the timing and frequency of parades was altered to make it easier for STC members to gain '*efficiency*'.

The suspension of Friday lectures was discontinued, again increasing the burden on cadets but there was some compensation; those who obtained Certificates A and B and satisfactory reports from the Commanding Officer would qualify for direct entry to an Officer Cadet Training Unit.[26]

In September, all cadets were required to sign the Home Guard

Enrolment Form in order to regularise *'the position of cadets if they are employed on operational duties against the enemy'.*[27]

Early in 1942, the Artillery Sub-unit received a further allocation of guns and now had six guns and tractors, creating an accommodation problem which was solved by relocating the gun park from the rear to the front of High School Yards. A record number of candidates (238) sat the Certificate B examinations and 232 passed. The following year 117 cadets gained Certificate B and in 1944 a further 149.

In 1943, Hamish Smith (Bsc Hons Civil Engineering 1945) joined the STC:

I was brought up in Muthill where I learned piping at school.

My first involvement with the military apart from school cadets, was when I joined the Home Guard in 1941 at age 14 yrs. The CO was the local minister who had baptised me and therefore knew I was under age, but chose to ignore it. There were a number of POW camps in the area (one being Cultybraggan) and when prisoners escaped we were called out and I remember chasing after them up Glen Artney armed with a shotgun. It was only latterly that we were issued with rifles.

I matriculated at Edinburgh University in 1943 at age 16. There were 60 in engineering at the start of the year and 40 finished the course. Any exam failures along the way meant that you had to leave and be called up. At the end of the 1943–44 session we went on to a 4 terms per year system for expediency, so a week after completing my first year, I commenced the second. I graduated in 1945 with an honours degree, only 2 years and 4 months from the date of matriculation!

Joining the STC was obligatory for all male students and we didn't get any pay. When I enlisted we were lined up and any pipers or drummers were requested to stand forward. Thinking that being a piper would incur extra duties which would detract from my studies, I kept quiet. Later I found out that the training time would be the same so owned up that I was a piper and got a hell of a dressing down for not saying so when asked initially.

*All cadets had to report to High School Yards for 4 hours train-
ing every Wednesday at 1.00pm. I lived in Cowan House which
had formal dining every evening and if you were late, which
sometimes happened after STC training, you got no meal. We
also had some training at weekends. Field training took place
in a specially allocated exercise area up Liberton Brae. Much
emphasis was put on drill and distance marching. Half of us
would march to the exercise area in platoons with a piper allocated to each platoon while the other half went by bus. Then
the initial marchers would come back by bus and the others
would march back. When I was piping I would play 6/8s fast
and had them running. Each platoon was allocated an invalided
Regular officer back from the front, supposedly on light duties
training cadets, and they didn't appreciate 'running'.*

*I remember becoming particularly adept at stripping and re-
assembling Bren guns interspersed with chanter practice. Everyone did infantry training and was expected to pass Cert B. All
piping instruction was from Pipe Major Jimmy Campbell who
was a medical student. We did have some instruction from a retired army pipe major but in highland dancing, not piping. I don't
recall his name but he was a large man weighing in at between
18 and 20 stone and for all that was surprisingly light on his feet.*

*We conducted many parades to raise money for the war ef-
fort, one specific cause being to pay for Hurricanes and Spit-
fires. Parades would take place along Princes Street with salutes
at the Mound and on the Castle Esplanade with Beating of Re-
treats. With so many public performances we were constantly
learning new tunes to maintain a varied repertoire and had to
remember a lot of sets. Life didn't always flow smoothly! Once
we were playing along Princes Street when Pipey Campbell
called the next set to play and then started to play a different
one. The pipers were 4 square, i.e. four ranks of four. I was in
one of the rearmost ranks and was aware of the most incredibly
discordant cacophony of sound until the band eventually realised what had happened and gradually switched to the new
set that the front rank was playing.*

Hamish was in the band when they performed Beating Retreat at Holyrood Palace on 25th May 1944 and two days later on the Castle Esplanade, where they were inspected by Lt Gen Andrew Thorne, KCB CMG DSO, GOC Scottish Command and Governor of Edinburgh Castle.

During June, July and August 1944, all 1st and 2nd year medical students in the STC acted as stretcher-bearers for the frequent ambulance trains arriving at Waverley Station with casualties from Hitler's V-1 and V-2 rocket bomb raids on London. Their work attracted high praise from the Department of Health and from railway officials, but, as the CO reported to the MEC:

> *It is regretted that this valuable work came to an abrupt halt when national service was placed on a voluntary basis and the majority of these cadets left the Corps.*

In the autumn, the Ministry of Labour and National Service relaxed the rules surrounding students' reserved status and it was no longer compulsory for them to serve in the STC. This resulted in a mass exodus, particularly from the Medical Sub-unit.

In October, Iain Maclaren (MB ChB 1949 FRCS Ed 1955) joined the STC:

> *I entered Edinburgh University Faculty of Medicine as a fresher in the first week of October 1944 having left school (Fettes College) in July aged 17.*
>
> *Although World War II was approaching its horrific climax, medical students were exempted from military service until graduation, but were obliged to serve in the University Senior Training Corps (STC), which formed a contingent of the Edinburgh Home Guard, or in some other organization involved in national defence at home in the United Kingdom.*
>
> *At some time before October 1944, this requirement had been abolished and a large proportion of the medical students resigned from the STC. At school, I had been a keen member of the JTC Pipe Band and I hoped to continue with this activity as*

a University student. Accordingly, I enrolled in the EUSTC as a Piper Cadet in late October 1944 and attended at the Quartermaster's Stores in High School Yards where I was issued with standard khaki battledress and a web belt but no other equipment.

A few days later I was kitted out with the OTC/STC pre-war pipe-band full dress uniform which was quite elaborate and significantly 'grander' than what was worn by Army bands at that time. It really was quite impressive and the kit that I received fitted me reasonably well so that I could justifiably take some pride in wearing it on ceremonial occasions.

Because of the pressures of study, I resigned from the STC in October 1946. I don't recall doing any military training during my two years as a Piper-Cadet, no fieldcraft or weapon training or anything like that. I did not attend any camps or field days but we did have drill parades to be 'smartened up' before public performances on the numerous ceremonial occasions.

Lt Col Moffat reported to the MEC and Senate that:

The results obtained from training have been very good indeed in all units except the Medical Unit where they have been most unsatisfactory owing to the almost complete lack of response from the Cadets.

He went on to explain that, because STC service had been compulsory, there were many cadets who would not otherwise have joined. For them, the Medical Unit was the branch of choice since it did little physical or military training and this explained both the high number of cadets in it (361) and the low efficiency rate, (only 65 cadets or 18%). At a meeting on 7th November 1944, the MEC unanimously decided, '*after hearing reports on the inefficiency of the cadets in the Medical Unit, that this unit should be disbanded*', and the Convener was asked to consult with the Dean of the Faculty of Medicine before submitting formal application to the WO.

Maxim machine-gun team in Old College
Quadrangle *c.* 1904.
CEUOTC

The first Edinburgh OTC Camp, Medical Division, Aldershot, 1908.
CEUOTC

Above: RE Unit, captioned
'Chaham Dene', believed to
be Chattenden, 1912.

University of Edinburgh PR
Department

Right: Colour Sergeant
Pringle-Pattison models the
new unifrom adopted by
the Infantry Sub-unit in
1913.

Edinburgh University Library,
Special Collections and
Archives, Acc. 1999/017

Artillery gun-team with Ordnance QF18-pounder Mk I, *c.*1914.

Edinburgh University Library, Special Collections and Archives,
Acc. 1999/017

Maxim Gun Team, Stobs Camp, 1914.

Edinburgh University Library, Special Collections and Archives,
Acc. 1999/017

Above: RE Unit, Carlingnose, North Queensferry, 1914.
University of Edinburgh PR Department

Below: Annual Camp, Peebles, 1915. From left Lt (later Captain) R.Gentles, Lt Gemmel, Major J.E. Mackenzie, 2/Lt (later Major) R. Kerr. John Mackenzie commanded the RA Unit, ran the 1915 Schools of Instruction, was Acting Adjutant throughout WWI. After the war he edited the University of Edinburgh *Roll of Honour*.
Edinburgh University Library, Special Collections and Archives,
Acc. 199/017

Above: Captain Kerr and RAMC and Infantry cadets on Isle of Man ferry, 1923.

Below: Annual Camp 1923. Infantry, Medical and Engineer Sub-units and Pipe Band disembark ferry at Douglas, Isle of Man. On the left is Major C.O.D. Preston DSO.

Edinburgh University Library, Special Collections and Archives, Acc. 1999/017

RE Unit, 'Barrel-piering' Hawick, 1923.
University of Edinburgh PR Department

Bisley winners, 1931.
OTC

RA 18-pounders live-firing, Redesdale, 1934.
University of Edinburgh PR Department

RA Unit, Redesdale, 1934.
University of Edinburgh PR Department

Armistice Day 1944, High School Yards

Iain Maclaren

Pipes & Drums, High School Yards 1944. Lt Col F J C Moffat DSO, front row centre. Capt W H Niven, Adjutant, third from left. RSM T W Darling third from right, Piper I F McLaren, front row, second from right.

Yerbury

The disbanding of the Medical Sub-unit reduced the Unit's strength from its all-time high of 1,066 to 705 cadets. In addition to the Commanding Officer, there were six regular officers (Adjutant, QM and the OCs of the Artillery, Engineer, Infantry and Signals Sub-units) and 17 TA officers, eleven of whom were members of staff at University of Edinburgh, one at Heriot-Watt, one at the Royal Infirmary and four 2/Lts who were undergraduates.

The Unit paraded at High School Yards on Armistice Day and took part in a major parade along Princes Street on 3rd December 1944 to mark the standing-down of the Home Guard. The salute was taken by General Sir Andrew Thorne and *The Scotsman* reported that it took 35 minutes for the parade to pass him.

In 1945, with the war in Europe over and that in the Far East coming to an end, cadet numbers dropped sharply across the country and in an effort to boost recruitment, the training requirement to gain efficiency was reduced to 30 training periods of at least 45 minutes each plus at least ten days at camp and an annual weapons training course, although medical students in their clinical years were exempted the latter. However, this had little impact; as former Cadet Piper Iain Maclaren put it: '*At the end of the war, everyone disappeared: there was only the Pipe Band left!*'

This was almost literally correct in the case of the Infantry Sub-unit; the more technical arms were also affected but to a lesser degree.

At the start of the first training year after the war, Col A. D. B. Smith (He was gazetted as A. D. B. Smith but was more usually known as A. D. Buchanan-Smith) took over from Frank Moffat as Commanding Officer and the WO introduced a fundamental change in the objective of cadet training and, hence, in its nature. The emphasis was now to be on personal development and leadership skills.

As the CO explained in a report to Senate: '*The majority of young men who now come to the University possess most of those qualities which are required of an officer, but their talent for leadership is frequently wholly dormant*'. Training for Certificates A and B was to be a secondary objective but '*not unimportant, since a leader must be skilled in the technicalities of his job'.*

Two new Sub-units were established, REME (Royal Electrical and Mechanical Engineers) and Intelligence Corps, and a new programme of training was introduced. Military and technical training would be conducted throughout the year at the drill hall in High School Yards and Sub-units would attend Easter attachments, typically of around ten days although this varied, to a Regular Army Unit or Depot of their arm. Summer camp was for the whole Unit where the training would be less military and include, for example, navigation exercises in the Highlands with initiative tests and challenges thrown in. Other options were available and in 1945 some of the more ambitious cadets availed themselves of an opportunity to undertake a commando course at Achnacarry while others spent the Christmas holiday on a mountaineering course in the Cairngorms. This winter adventure training became an annual event.

The Unit's first formal engagement after the war was the provision of a Guard of Honour at the McEwan Hall on 26th November 1945 when General Dwight D. Eisenhower, the former Supreme Commander of Allied Forces in Europe during the last year of WWII and a future President of the United States, was awarded an honorary degree.

In June 1946, the STC conducted a rare combined operation with the University Naval Division and the University Air Squadron (UAS). Using three landing craft borrowed from Rosyth Naval base, the naval cadets transported the Infantry Sub-unit to carry out an offensive landing on the island of Inchkeith in the Firth of Forth. En route they evaded a 'torpedo attack' with the deployment of a smokescreen and air support provided by the UAS and after successful land operations, were ferried back to the fishing harbour of Newhaven in Edinburgh, where the quaint seafront bars no doubt enjoyed a sharp but short-lived rise in beer sales.

In October, the Unit again paraded with the Pipe Band at the McEwan Hall to provide a Guard of Honour at the installation of The Marquess of Linlithgow as Chancellor of the University and for the conferral of an honorary degree to Field Marshall the Rt Hon. Viscount Montgomery of Alamein GCB, DSO, Chief of the

Imperial General Staff. Viscount Montgomery and the new Chancellor, who was also Honorary Colonel of Edinburgh STC, inspected the parade.

The 1947, Easter Attachments were typical. The gunners went to The School of Artillery at Larkhill, the Engineers to Lockerbie and the Signals to the War Office Communications Centre in London, followed by twelve days at Catterick.

The Contingent summer camp was at Dunbar, which served as a base from which cadets went out on a series of short exercises and initiative tests ranging over southern Scotland and to which they returned *as required for hot meals, dry clothes, dances and demonstrations*.

Finances at this time were a cause for major concern. Cadets who had joined during the war were coming to the end of their university course and leaving, but few of the new intakes of students had any interest in joining the STC. By September 1947, strength was down to 114, of whom only 56 were efficient and by the following year was just 33, the lowest in the Contingent's entire history. The consequent drop in the WO annual per capita grant almost forced the Unit to close, but it was saved by a special grant of £750 from the Treasury that enabled it to *continue on an austerity basis*.

The Pipe Band, despite always been at or near proper strength, suffered from the lack of funds. The Macfarlane tartan kilts (which it had worn since its formation in 1909) were no longer available and could not be afforded privately. It switched to Hunting Stuart kilts provided by 7/9 Bn Royal Scots.

On 1st April 1948, the Corps was renamed the University Training Corps (UTC) and became part of the Territorial Army although cadets, by concession, were not liable for mobilisation. Another significant change was that an efficient cadet who passed the Officer Selection Board would go straight to an Officer Training Unit instead of doing the normal preliminary training, much of which would have been a repetition of the UTC syllabus.

On 1st February 1949, the Women's Royal Army Corps was formed, replacing the ATS (Auxiliary Territorial Service) and in November the MEC advised Senate that it wished to form a WRAC Sub-unit. Authority was given by the WO and a University Company was formed in 1950 as part of 314 Battalion, WRAC. In effect, this was the first time that women were admitted to the OTC but it would be some years before that became their formal status.

The Pipe Band had a particularly successful year; it won the Inter-University Pipe Band Competition and individual members were 1st and 2nd in the individual piping and 1st, 2nd and 3rd in the individual drumming.

The Training Major at this time was Major A. R. G Pringle-Pattison, Queen's Own Cameron Highlanders, who was to die in action in Tel-el-Kabir in 1952, shortly after leaving the Unit.

In 1950, the WO approved the design for new UTC cap-badge but declined to give official recognition, and hence funding, for the Pipe Band. The Band had enjoyed official recognition for many years from 1909 and it is not clear when this was withdrawn. However, as the lack of funding was a significant issue and this was the first recorded objection by the MEC, it seems probable that the change in status was during or shortly after WWII.

In May 1951, a meeting of all Scottish UTCs had determined three proposals to be put to the WO:

1) *All Scottish Sub-units should wear highland uniform regardless of arm.* [This was a majority decision not supported by Edinburgh.]

2) *Parachute training should be available to UTC cadets.*

3) *Pipe Bands should be officially recognised.*

There is no record of the WO response, but it seems that approval was not given to any of the proposals.

From 1st October 1952, the WRAC Company became a Sub-unit of the UTC and the following year several notable events occurred.

In the summer, the Pipe Band again won the Inter-University Pipe Band Competition, but it was reported to the MEC that it had been the only band wearing khaki. Aberdeen UTC had been wearing new No. 1 dress paid for by the University of Aberdeen and the MEC agreed to present a request to the University of Edinburgh for a grant to attire the Edinburgh band similarly. Circumstantial evidence suggests that the grant was given.

In the autumn, Col Smith relinquished command, retiring with the honorary rank of Brigadier, and was succeeded by Lt Col W. A. Sinclair. Captain Giles, who had commanded the WRAC Company since its formation, also stood down and was replaced by Captain F. E. Barfoed who would command the Sub-unit until its disbandment.

HRH The Duke of Edinburgh was appointed Honorary Colonel in succession to the Marquess of Linlithgow, who had held the appointment for 20 years. It was hoped that the new Honorary Colonel would visit the Unit when at the University in November for his installation as Chancellor, but this was precluded by his tight programme. However, the Unit did parade and provide a Guard of Honour.

There was an issue over accommodation. The space the UTC occupied in High School Yards was required for the expansion of academic departments, but the alternative offered, the New College Settlement premises in the Pleasance, were not suitable. Not only were they significantly smaller and would require much modification, but there was no room for a parade ground and three sides of the building were on public roads giving rise to security problems which, for a military base, were considered insuperable.

In 1954, ten officers and 96 cadets as usual attended Easter Attachments with various Regular Schools and Units and the Victoria weekend was at Otterburn. On this occasion, a notable milestone was achieved in the Artillery Sub-unit with the cadets themselves performing all roles on the gun position. Instead of merely manning the guns, cadets acted as Gun Position Officer (in command of the firing), Command Post Officer (who monitored communications with the Forward Observation Officers and the work of the plotters, and passed the orders to the guns), radio-operator and TARAs (Technical Assistants RA, the plotters who calculated the settings for the gun-sights).

In May, a conference of the Commanding Officers and Training Officers of all UK UTC Contingents was hosted by the University of Edinburgh and addressed by the Principal. The conference determined eleven proposals. While most were essentially administrative, three were noteworthy:

1) The role of UTCs to be 'Giving basic military training, in appropriate arms; developing leadership; and providing suitable training for junior officers'.

2) The designation to be 'Officers Training Corps'.

3) The syllabus to be as at present but with greater emphasis on leadership training.

It was also proposed that the organisation of Sub-units continue unchanged, cadets were not to wear Officer-Cadet insignia, their pay rates were to remain as at present and all COs were to be Lt Cols regardless of the number of Sub-units. On this occasion, the WO did accede to some of the requests.

The thorny accommodation problem for Edinburgh UTC was also resolved. One of the TA units using the Forrest Road Drill Hall was to be relocated and the UTC would move in. It would be shared with another Unit but there would be no clash as training times differed.

In December, the Corps went to Glenmore for the tenth successive year, equipped with the latest army mountain warfare clothing and arctic tents. The camp, based in the Forestry Commission huts was commanded by Captain Rae, an experienced officer who had served in the 1939–45 war and was now a 4th year medical student, while training was to be run by Captain McIntosh, a 4th Year Veterinary student. Many of the cadets had been there previously and the routine was familiar. But this year was to be far from routine ... and tragic.

Chapter 5

A Decade
of Change

CAMP WAS QUICKLY and efficiently established with Headquarters and base in the Forestry huts and a tented camp high up the mountain on a spur at Coire-na-Ciste.

Lt Col Sinclair arrived on Monday 20th December to visit the cadets and, around midday on Tuesday, set out in clear weather with Captains Rae and McIntosh to climb to the tented camp. As they approached 2,000 feet (around 600 metres) a sudden blizzard blew up and visibility was reduced to less than 20 metres. They continued to climb and, around 3 pm, visibility improved briefly and they could see, ahead and below, Loch Avon and Strath Nethy. They had reached the col to the north-east of the summit of Cairngorm and realised that they had missed – and were now far beyond – the cairn at which they should have turned towards the camp. The fierce wind was bitterly cold and there was little more than an hour of daylight left. The CO decided that, rather than retracing their steps into the teeth of the blizzard, they would continue ahead and descend ahead into Strath Nethy to get some shelter from the wind and follow the path north to a ruined bothy and then west from there back to the Glenmore base.

As they descended, Sinclair was beginning to show signs of fatigue but they reached the path at about 4.15 pm and started slowly along the glen. At around 6 pm, the CO '*showed the first definite signs of collapse*' and the other officers had to assist him. Soon they were virtually carrying him and progress slowed even further.

After about an hour Rae and McIntosh realised the situation was becoming critical and that a different plan of action was required. They felt they must be near the ruined bothy at the north end of the Strath. Rae would stay with the CO while McIntosh would press on alone. If the bothy were within 300 yards, he would return and they would carry Sinclair to it. If it were not, he would continue on to the Glenmore huts and summon help. In fact, they were fully three miles from the bothy.

Meanwhile, the officer at the huts, having been informed by radio that the expected visitors had failed to arrive at the tented camp, organised parties to leave hot drinks and food at Jean's Hut and the Nethy bothy and to have a vehicle patrol the track between there and the huts.

Sinclair fell into a deep sleep from which he could not be wakened. Rae lifted the CO onto his back and kept moving his arms to try to keep him warm but this became more difficult as Rae himself got tired. Colonel Sinclair died at 9.30 pm.

Rae continued resuscitation attempts for an hour but without success. After a rest, he then set out at 11 pm to make his own way to Glenmore. He was picked up by the patrolling vehicle at 2.30 am and reached the huts at around 3 am where he learned that there had been no sign of Captain McIntosh. The RAF Mountain Rescue team at Kinloss were contacted and responded immediately, sending three teams of 16 men each, the first of which arrived at Glenmore at 5 am. The recovery of Lt Col Sinclair's body presented no difficulty but the search for Captain McIntosh was less straightforward. He was eventually found about midday some 300 yards north of the bothy and taken directly to Raigmore Hospital in Inverness '*badly bruised and suffering from extreme exposure and exhaustion*'. He had no recollection of events after leaving Sinclair and Rae and clearly owed his survival to the prompt response and diligence of the RAF teams.

A Military Court of Enquiry concluded that no blame could be attached to either Captains Rae or McIntosh and the '*bravery and courage*' of Captain Rae was specially noted and recorded.

Sinclair had been a distinguished lecturer in philosophy and had made a series of eight broadcasts between December 1939 and May 1940 on 'The Voice of the Nazi' and their propaganda machine, attracting the wrath of Hitler and Goebbels. He died one week short of his 49th birthday and had been married for only four months.

At an MEC meeting in June 1955, it was reported that the cadets wanted to erect a memorial to Colonel Sinclair. The original intention had been to site it at the spot where he died, but the landowner refused permission. However, Colonel Iain Grant of Rothiemurchus agreed to a shelter being built on his land beside the path through the Lairig Grhu.

Various Edinburgh companies donated material, including pre-cast concrete blocks, roofing girders and teak for doors and windows, and delivered it to 'Piccadilly' (a long-standing nickname for a junction of paths in Rothiemurchus Forest). This was a clearing in the woods around two miles south-east of Aviemore and was to be the base for operations during construction.

The Angus Sinclair Memorial Bothy was officially opened on 6th July 1957 with over 50 people in attendance. The Order of Service for the Ceremony carried the following description of the project:

The site was marked in May 1956 and a start was made with the block-carrying in August. This carrying continued at Christmas. The Sappers went up for Easter Training and, in addition to an intensive programme of carrying, excavated and concreted the base of the bothy. The following week a start was made with the walls but a heavy fall of snow stopped all work.

At the Victoria week-end the Sappers continued carrying and construction. Strong northerly winds with rain, hail and snow made work difficult and one night a section of wall was blown down. Despite this the walls were completed to about 4 feet. During another long week-end, 14th to 18th June, a small party continued the construction.

The Contingent moved up on 22nd June for Annual Training and by the 26th the roof was on and concreted over.

The site is above the 2,000 foot contour and approximately 16 tons of building material have been carried from the base at 'Piccadilly' up four miles of rough track. This represents over 700 man loads of about 50 lbs each, including difficult compo-

nents such as fifteen foot lengths of angle girder, doors and windows. In addition, about 25 tons of natural stone (mostly pink granite), gravel and sand have been collected or quarried on the site.

It is reckoned that the actual building has taken 16 days. The pre-cast concrete blocks were an important element. Carrying time was spread over about 35 days.

The work was all most carefully planned and has been treated as a military operation by the Sapper Sub-unit of the O.T.C. We owe a great deal to the foresight, energy and drive of their Commander, Major Norman Sidwell, PhD, of the Heriot Watt College.

This report implies that the Engineer Sub-unit had undertaken the entire project but members of other Sub-units had performed much of the carrying as former Infantry cadet, Private Nigel Malcolm-Smith recalls:

Our annual camp that year was at Loch-an-Eilein and we mixed our infantry training with carrying materials up to the bothy. It was really hard work. We carried breeze-blocks in rucksacks and would make a couple of trips a day ... quite a hump! The steel girders for the roof were heavy and awkward, about 15 feet long, and had to be carried by three men.

I attended the opening ceremony and there were well over fifty people there, of all ages. Pipers were stationed at intervals along the track up to the bothy to give some encouragement ...

One of those pipers was Pipe Corporal Ronnie Seiler:

We rose early and started up the hill carrying our pipes. There was no road or car park in those days but the path was fairly well laid out and there were good bridges over the burns and larger streams. When we reached the more open part of the route, individual pipers were deployed at intervals of about 800 yards. We were posted well away from the path and stood in knee high heather. As is often the case with the Army we were far too early and had to remain at our post in a very hot sun for about two to three hours. Eventually the VIP party appeared with quite a few of the more elderly on ponies. We knew they were approaching before we could see them by the sound of the pipes sounding off further down the valley when the top party appeared. I was the Pipe Corporal at the time and played second last. The Pipe Major, Hamish Nicolson, was last off. You finished the tune you were playing when you heard the next piper striking up then you struggled through the heather to rejoin the path and catch up with the VIPs.

When we eventually neared the Bothy we formed up, out of sight, below the area of flat land in front of the building and waited until the top party had got settled. At the given signal Hamish got us playing a march and started up a very steep slope covered in dense tangled heather to try and reach this flat area in front of the Bothy. With the pipers struggling, out of breath, stumbling and tripping, the noise we produced must have been fairly ragged and one by one we fell out, unable to go on playing our pipes. Indeed, it was all we could do to get up the hill at all what with our fairly heavy uniform, kilts and spats and all. The only one to make it over the brow of the hill still playing was Hamish himself. I think it was a superhuman effort and have nothing but praise for him. We eventually all struggled to the top, reformed as a band once we got our breath back and were able to play a fairly decent tune for the occasion.

Over the next 30 years, periodic visits were made to the bothy to carry out maintenance work and over time this became increasingly burdensome, both physically and financially, in part due to its age but latterly because of vandalism. By 1987, thoughts were turning to demolition and in 1989 the CO met Susan Sinclair, Angus's widow, who reluctantly accepted that the bothy should be demolished. This was carried out in the summer of 1991 and a memorial plaque mounted at the spot.

Following the death of Lt Col Sinclair, the Training Officer,

Major T. Little, MC KOSB assumed command as Acting CO until a successor could be appointed. There was no suitable candidate on the University staff and the MEC requested the local Territorial and Auxiliary Forces Association to try to identify a suitable TA officer. They were unable to do so and the Unit's first Regular Army CO, Lt Col D. I. H Callender RS, was appointed in November.

In the meantime, the WO had responded to some of the proposals made by the Commanding Officers following their conference in Edinburgh. The Corps was re-named the Officers Training Corps and the Pipe Band was officially recognised. Its uniform was to be kilts of the Hunting Stewart tartan and '*otherwise as for 7/9 Royal Scots apart from cap-badge and buttons*'.

In December 1955, the usual adventure training was undertaken in the Cairngorms and there was another accident:

> ### ONE SLIP – AND FIVE MEN PLUNGE 60ft
> #### On mountain where their CO died

ran the headline.[28]

Three officers and two cadets were descending a steep slope in single file when the third man lost his footing and slid into the two men in front, causing them to lose their balance. All three started careering down the snow-covered and boulder-strewn hillside. The two behind rushed to their aid but also fell. All five slithered and tumbled an estimated 60 feet (20 metres) before their slide was halted. Two of the officers had broken collarbones and the third had concussion and extensive bruising. Both cadets had minor back injuries which subsequently required hospitalisation but were able to make their way down to base at Glenmore and summon help for the officers who had taken shelter in Jean's Hut. A doctor from Aviemore went up to the hut to treat the injured while an RAF mountain-rescue team set out from Kinloss. The three officers were carried down on stretchers.

Although this incident was not nearly as severe as that the previous year, Senate were dismayed and on 30th January 1956 the University Secretary wrote to the MEC expressing their '*grave concern*' and recommending:

that members of the University Training Corps ought to be med-
ically examined before taking part in such training, and that
they should receive preliminary instruction in climbing and be
adequately hardened up before the training period, that they
should make proper use of mountaineering equipment, and that
parties should be led by experienced mountaineers with a
knowledge of the region.

While Senate's sentiments and intentions were well-intentioned and had the interests of their students at heart, this letter had obviously been written without any attempt to establish the actual circumstance beyond the mere fact that there had been two accidents. The MEC minutes merely record that, at a meeting on 5th March, the letter was discussed at considerable length. As the recommendations themselves were simplistic they would have occasioned no debate and it can be assumed that the deliberations were on how to respond to such a high-handed and patronising letter. In the event, the convener, former CO Brigadier A. D. Buchanan-Smith replied to the University Secretary on the 12th. While his reply was in measured tones, it is clear that each recommendation was regarded as an unfounded criticism and each was thoroughly countered by a simple statement of the facts, such as the rigorous and constant medical assessment by an RAMC doctor with the group and the fact that they had been equipped with the latest winter equipment as issued to the Royal Marines. There was no further communication from the University on the matter.

While the MEC was handling these 'politics', the Unit continued with its routine training programmes, but changes were in the offing.

In 1956, the WO withdrew the Intelligence and REME Sub-units and conversion work was carried out on the Forrest Road Drill Hall, aided by grants from the University totalling £3,000. In May 1957 the Unit relocated there from High School Yards.

In 1958, cadets were granted the status of Officer Cadets (OCdt) and henceforth wore appropriate insignia, either a white band on their epaulettes or white cords or gorgettes on their collars, depending on uniform. In February the Unit was visited by the Honorary Colonel and in July participated in a parade at Holyrood Park to mark the 50th anniversary of the Territorial Army. In November, Lt Col C. S. Campbell MC TD, who had previously served as a cadet in the Artillery Sub-unit and served in the Royal Artillery in WWII, took over command.

On 14th January 1959, the WO wrote to Units giving a new rank and pay scheme and followed this on 3rd February with a new syllabus for Certificate B, which, it was estimated, would take at least two years to complete. The combined effect was a reduction in Officer Cadets' pay by about 2/- per day with no prospect of earning the full (Certificate B) increment until near the end of the average service period of three years. These arrangements were met with dismay, noting that the Pipe Band, *'the most enthusiastic Unit'* and the one with the fullest training programme, could not possibly *'do such an elaborate Certificate B'*. The CO reported to the MEC that he thought it would be difficult to maintain enthusiasm for a qualification that was *'so far ahead'*, particularly since Cadets could get a TA commission without the certificate.

Around this time, the Unit received several requests from local TA Units for officers, this being noted by the CO and MEC as an indication that the OTC was generally regarded as an *'officer-producing Unit'*, exactly as the WO intended.

On Friday 22nd May, 126 people attended a Centenary Dinner in the University Union. This function was presided over by General Sir Philip Christison, grandson of Professor Robert Christison who had chaired the meeting of students and staff on 24th May 1859 when the University Volunteer Company had been raised.

On Sunday 24th 1959, the actual centenary, the Pipe Band performed Beating Retreat in the University's Old College quadrangle and a sherry party was held in the Playfair Library from where the guests could gaze out over to the classroom where the 1859 meeting was reputed to have been held. (In an article in the 'Medical History' section of an unidentified journal, Sir Philip stated that too many men had attended the original meeting to be accommodated in the classroom and that they had moved to the quadrangle where Sir Robert addressed them from the steps.)

The WRAC Sub-unit had by now established an enviable reputation. It had dominated the Inter-University Country Dancing Cup competition for several years and again won it in 1959. In addition, it won the Command Drill Competition (the first OTC Unit to do so) and the Command Inter-Unit Shooting Competition. In 1960 they again won the Inter-University and Command Dancing competitions as well as the Command Shooting and Table Tennis trophies.

As anticipated, the new, onerous Certificate B syllabus proved to be a deterrent and by 1960 attendance was falling off badly. The CO proposed to discontinue the formal training for the Certificate and focus on leadership training for the majority. For the few Officer Cadets who did want to do the certificate, the information was readily available. This was a shrewd move and attendances improved.

In September 1960, the WO caused outrage in the OTC, COMEC, MECs and their associated Universities. The Director of the Territorial Army and an Air Ministry representative bluntly announced to the annual meeting of COMEC that the future of University Service Units would depend on their output of Regular officers. Furthermore, unless the target was reached within one year, OTCs might be closed down!

This was universally seen as completely contrary to the historical purpose of OTCs and the high-handed, threatening manner of its intimation was considered grossly discourteous to the academic partners in the OTC contract. Edinburgh MEC felt so strongly about the issue that if no official objection were to be sent by COMEC, then one should certainly be sent the University of Edinburgh. Furthermore, if the production of an annual quota of Regular officers, which was seen as a recruitment role, were to be mandatory, the University might even choose to close the service units.

Formal objections were submitted to the WO but there was no ready solution in sight. Then, at an Edinburgh MEC meeting on 5th June 1961, Professor T. B. Smith reported that an opportunity had arisen at a dinner in Edinburgh to mention the problem of the future of OTCs to the Prime Minister, who had asked to be more fully briefed. The Principal then wrote to the PM. Separately, the CO told the MEC that he understood from contacts in the MoD that the Minister and the Army itself were strongly in favour of the continuance of the OTC, but some senior civil servants were not. This was a situation that would be repeated in the decades ahead, but for the moment developments were awaited.

In the meantime, the CO felt that cadet numbers (260) were now such that it was possible to have a full parade, but that the appearance would be improved if all men wore the same uniform instead of the distinctive uniforms of the different Sub-units. The 7/9th Royal Scots were about to cease wearing their Hunting Stewart kilts (as already worn by the OTC Pipe Band) and the WO approved their transfer to the OTC. Henceforth they would be issued to all male Officer Cadets for ceremonial occasions. As the WRAC cadets had to buy their own tartan skirts, they would continue to wear Black Watch tartan.

The WO position on the future of the OTC had softened (or they had won their argument with the Civil Service). At the COMEC annual meeting in London on 9th December 1961, Major-General C. M. F. Deakin, Director Territorial Army, proposed that the role of the OTC be amended to be:

(a) *to provide a practical link between Service thought and the Universities, thereby fostering interest in the Military affair of the nation and in the Army as one of the instruments in the policy of national defence;*

(b) *to provide pre-service training for those graduates who consider joining the Regular Army;*

(c) *to provide pre-service training for candidates for commissions in the Army Emergency Reserve, in the Territorial Army and in the Combined Cadet Force.*

The three parts of the role are regarded as equally important.

This was approved unanimously.

He then put forward for discussion several possible areas for economies, emphasizing that no action would be taken without prior discussion with MECs:

(a) *Contingents which are below strength would be disbanded;*

(b) *Reduction in establishment, making entry more difficult, even competitive;*

(c) *The number of Sub-units be reduced to five for larger contingents and three for others;*

(d) *Pay for officer cadets to be brought into line with other officer cadets;*

(e) *Savings on camps e.g. abolished, shortened, alternate years or 'Greenfield' only;*

(f) *Camps centralised so that several contingents camp together.*

The meeting readily agreed point (d) and, in the face of strong objections, (e) was dropped. Considerable discussion ensued on the other suggestions, with no clear decisions reached.[29]

On the 19th November 1962, the WO wrote to Commanding Officers announcing some changes and bringing pay into line with non-OTC Officer Cadets, namely 13/3d per day for men and 11/3d for women. For those holding Certificate B and the CO's recommendation, the rates were 16/9d and 14/3d. From 1st April 1963 these would rise to 14/- (12/-) and 17/6d (15/-). [To give this some context, a pint of beer in a normal pub cost around 1/- at that time.] However, with immediate effect no cadets were to be promoted to provisional or substantive NCO or Warrant rank, although any already holding such ranks substantively would continue to do so until they left the OTC. All members apart from officers would have the substantive rank of Officer Cadet. COs did however have authority to appoint cadets to Cadet NCO ranks or as Senior or Junior Under Officers but this would be a purely local arrangement and would attract no increase in pay.[30]

This was against a background where the Treasury was still questioning the value of the OTC. At a Cabinet meeting on 29th November, the Chief Secretary of the Treasury argued that the OTCs cost around half a million pounds, produced too few Regular Officers and should be closed down. The MOD responded that this was not their sole [*sic*] role and that, since a significant element of the cost was for Regular staff, only half of the cost could be saved.

The First Secretary of State (Rab Butler) was in favour of retaining the OTC and the Prime Minister voiced two options:

1) *To continue with the present lack of policy and consequent uncertainty for a year or so, then close down, or*

2) *To give firm support and encourage universities to make more of the OTC.*

Happily, the Cabinet favoured the latter[31] but another surprise was in the offing.

In March 1963, the Convener of the MEC received a letter from the WO announcing to his '*complete and utter surprise*' that the WRAC Sub-units would be disbanded at the end of the current academic year. The four Scottish universities and Queen's Belfast had the strongest WRAC Sub-units and the MEC felt '*that any protest would have to be made on a nationalistic basis by these five*', but only after the decision had been formally announced by Parliament. The COMEC Executive made strong representations at a high level against the proposal and several Universities, including Edinburgh, formally protested, but to no avail. Captain Barfoed had received no prior information or instructions, her Permanent Staff were simply posted away.

A farewell dinner to the WRAC Sub-unit was held on 14th June in the Students' Union.

Chapter 6

Skottetoget: The Scottish March in Norway

ANNUAL CAMP IN 1963 was exceptional, an imaginative concept devised by the CO, Lt Col Charles Campbell MC TD and described by Lord Balerno (formerly Brigadier A. D. Buchanan-Smith) as *'possibly the most outstanding event that has ever happened to the OTC'*. Given the high profile at the time, and to this day in the memories of the Officer-Cadets who participated, it is possible to record it in detail.

In August 1612 a group of around 300 Scottish mercenaries had sailed from Caithness to join the Swedish Army of Gustavus Adolphus. As the Danes controlled the only suitable Swedish port, the Scots landed at Andalsnes in Norway and began an overland trek towards Sweden. Although they behaved properly towards the Norwegian people and property they encountered, they were betrayed by one of their local guides and on 26th August, at Kringen, about 100 miles from the coast, were ambushed by local militia and most were killed. Of 134 taken prisoner, all but a handful were murdered the following day. Some reports say that most had been unarmed as they expected to be equipped by the Swedes, but this is unlikely.

Four officers were captured and sent to Oslo. Presumably thinking they might be treated more leniently if they were not seen to have been in command, they said that a Company Commander who had been killed in the ambush, Sinclair, was the leader, and the whole affair has gone down in history as the Sinclair March. The four officers were repatriated.

Over 350 years later, Col Campbell's plan was to re-enact the Sinclair March.

Former Officer-Cadet Douglas Proudlock takes up the story:

> *As I understand it, Charlie Campbell (the CO) got himself invited to the reception for the first Mountbatten lecture given at the University by laying on a Guard of Honour. At the reception he buttonholed the Duke of Edinburgh, the then Chancellor, and asked for his support for the Norway trip. He made a similar request of Lord Mountbatten for the Navy's support and got agreement there as well. Shortly afterwards the story goes that Charlie repeated the Guard of Honour routine when King Olav paid a state visit to Edinburgh and visited the University. Charlie now had the support of the King and therefore a fair amount of ammunition to fire at the army bureaucracy who were obliged to lend their support.*

The WO approved the plan provided there was no cost to the public.

Any annual camp required considerable planning; to prepare for one overseas where the Contingent would need to be largely self-sufficient, and to do so at no extra cost, was ambitious to say the least. A large quantity and variety of equipment had to be organised and loaded on the vehicles and this work started weeks before departure. Former Officer-Cadet David Bayne (BL 1962), who would go on the command the Unit in 1978–80 saw for himself:

> *I happened to be in the Unit stores ten days before departure when three members of the WRAC came in and asked to collect the 'three seat thunderbox'. The civilian quartermaster at that time was John Forbes, a 'character' by any set of criteria. 'Would you please turn round, ladies?' he asked, and when they had done so he said 'Yep, I have the correct size, six and seven-eighths'. More seriously, this was the first insight I had into the massive logistical exercise behind the trip to Norway.*

However, the hurdles were all crossed and a plan came together. An Edinburgh shipping company, Salvesens, had strong Norwegian connections and would transport the vehicles to and from Norway free of charge. The Royal Navy would take the Officer Cadets from Rosyth in HMS *Plover*, a minelayer, but had no accommodation for females so the WRAC Sub-unit would be flown out by the Royal Norwegian Air Force.

On 24th June, the WRAC went to Edinburgh airport while the main party moved to Rosyth. Unfortunately, HMS *Plover* had developed an engine fault and was delayed indefinitely but the women, ostensibly trusting the Navy to sort thing out – but more likely unwilling to delay the adventure – left as planned. The Royal Navy did sort things out, diverting the RFA Tanker *Wave Chief*. After a smooth crossing, the main party arrived in the picturesque Andalsnesfjord and disembarked on the morning of 27th. From the East Quay, they marched through the town, past the Mayor to the camp and immediately embarked on a programme arranged by the townsfolk, including sightseeing, sports and shooting competitions and a folklore festival.

Former Officer-Cadet Sheena McKelvie (BSc 1963, DipEd 1964, now Gillespie) describes the festival, which was to be repeated at every town stopover:

> *The WRAC did not take part in the actual march or participate in any of the parades – Capt Barfoed cosseted her girls, and we did not do that sort of thing! However, we did take a full part in all the cultural activities along the route. At most places we had folk dancing, and we had a dancing team in white dresses and sashes who did some Scottish country dances. Some of the men sang, or recited poems, and there was some contribution from the Norwegians – usually dancing – in their national costume.*

The Pipe Band performed Beating Retreat in front of the Grand Hotel and at an official luncheon the CO was presented with a commemorative wood-carving.

All too soon it was time to start the actual march. The Contingent was divided into four groups, each completely self-contained and with their own dedicated transport. A and B Groups were the marchers, C Group was the WRAC while the fourth Group comprised Main HQ and the Pipes and Drums.

On Sunday 30th June the marchers set off on the first 20-mile stage. Meanwhile, the rest of the party travelled to Dombas where the WRAC would stay in a Norwegian Army School until the move to Oslo. Their role was to provide logistical support, driving the vehicles and delivering supplies to the men on the actual march and setting up the camps: several of the men have commented on what a marvellous job they did. The marchers arrived on 1st July in time for another folklore festival.

David Bayne:

The big day came along soon enough. We were split into two groups of about platoon strength, each platoon with three sections of around ten cadets. Each day would see a 'Platoon Sergeant' appointed and there would be a morning and afternoon section leader appointed. The march was not just to be a long walk, it was going to be an assessment as well. Dress was shirt-sleeve order with 39-pattern webbing minus large pack and the pipers took turns in accompanying a platoon for a day.

With spirits high, off we stepped. Within a very short time, several factors emerged. The ammunition boot, with its steel heel and tackety leather sole, gave a most satisfying crunch as one marched and made it easy to stay in step and develop a rhythm. But it was made of very stiff leather and unless it was a very good fit, blisters were going to be a problem. Then there was the heat and sun; it was Norway's hottest summer of the century and very few of us had any experience of such conditions and no-one carried any sun-block. Along with the heat, came the mosquitos. Now, I will yield to no-one in my respect for, and awe of, the fire-power of the Scottish West Highland midge, but I reckon the Norwegian mosquito would put up quite a fight in the battle for air supremacy!

Officer-Cadet George Livingstone-Learmonth (BSc Natural Sciences 1965):

We wore kilts with army shirts with sleeves rolled up. Norway had a heat wave on so it was incredibly hot and most people got sunburnt on their forehead, wrists, back of the neck and on the back of the knees in the gap between the top of the green highland stockings and the bottom of the kilt. All except Dave Simpson that is, who took his shirt off for 20 minutes during our first stop for lunch, and in the crystal clear air soon turned scarlet and made such a noise a couple of hours later that he was put in the support truck for the rest of the day and had special dispensation not to wear any straps over his shoulders for the remainder of the march. A few days later he made a terrible fuss again when his skin peeled and he itched so badly he couldn't stand still for a moment or march in a straight line.

Much of the time we had the pipes playing as we marched, sometimes the full band, and sometimes just a few pipers or just the one like Robin McKinley as we strode along in the open country. 'Scotland the Brave' and all the old favourites were belted out, and we got so used to the music that even when none was being played you could still hear the pipes in your head resounding far away up in the hills through which we were passing.

A rather concerned individual called Denis was with us, who allegedly had being trying to gain a commission for some time and had finally managed it just before we went to Norway, and this was his first outing as an officer. Of course, as the pipes were playing we often joined in and much rousing singing took place amongst the troops as we went along. Unfortunately for Denis when all other words failed the favourite rendition was: 'There's no one quite like him – or more we adore (abhor?) – than Denis the Menace – The cow-punchers whore'. Despite all his best efforts Denis never could suppress the enthusiasm of the troops for their vocals.

Officer-Cadet Scott Lindsay (BSc 1966) was appointed piper for A Company on 1st July:

Robin (OCdt Robin Mackinlay) and I set off in an Austin Champ to join the main group as it was our turn to march. I was dropped with A Group under Captain Brownlow A&SH (TA). We went about 20 miles in the scorching sun altogether and I managed to keep up a fairly constant flow of tunes. The pace was short and quick which didn't suit me. Fortunately, it didn't suit Captain Brownlow either, having long legs like myself, so in between tunes we marched in our own time at the front.

We had a good singer, O/Cdt George Fleming, who led some rousing songs on the march. A favourite was 'The Bonnie Lass o' Fyvie-o' which I adapted to play on the pipes and it became the unofficial theme song.

On 2nd July, rather than marching in the heat, the main parties rested while HQ and the band moved to the picturesque little town of Otta, situated at the confluence of two rivers and surrounded by hills. This was half a mile from Kringen, the site of the ambush, and was the main base at the end of the march.

George Livingston-Learmonth:

After three days of marching in the heat our Colonel decided it was just too darn hot and so decided we should break the back of the remaining mileage by marching through the night – we would start again just before midnight. Of course being young and fit every one rose to the challenge and march all night we did – with the pipes blasting away as usual – even in villages through which we passed during the night – with the usual spirited vocals for much of the time. It was much easier in the cool of the night and everyone enjoyed it except poor Denis – who usually enjoyed marching along at the front of the column with his chest thrown out – but for this march the Colonel gave him a large red light and told him to march along at the back.

On the morning of 4th July, after two nights marching, A and B Groups were welcomed at Otta by the Pipes and Drums. As the Contingent marched through the town to the camp, the salute was again taken by the Mayor and the local children's band joined the parade for the last mile or so.

They also met up with a group of Officer-Cadets who had been delayed by exams. Alasdair Geater (MA 1963 LLB 1965) recalls:

About a dozen of us, medical and law students for the most part, had exams later than the day the annual camp started. We assembled at Waverley Station, took a train to South Shields, where we embarked on the overnight ferry to Bergen via Stavanger. From there, we took Norwegian Railways to Otta, arriving the day before the main body on foot.

To quote from the official report presented to the MEC:

That evening the SINCLAIR saga was relived when a hundred women ambushed the camp and bore their captives off to a party at KVAM, a village some fifteen miles to the south.

The following morning the Contingent paraded at the Sinclair Memorial at Prillarguri where it was inspected and addressed by Major-General Pran, Commander of Eastern District of the Norwegian Army who also presented a memento to Col Campbell. The General then joined the Contingent for lunch at the campsite together with the British Military Attaché from Oslo. In the evening a barbecue and dance was held at the camp to which a number of townspeople were invited.

The following day was more relaxed, devoted to sightseeing, including a visit to Sinclair's grave at Kvam.

On Sunday 7th, the Unit paraded with a Contingent from the Norwegian Army at a memorial in Kvam to men of The Green Howards and The York and Lancaster Regiment killed fighting the Germans in 1940. A drumhead service was held and wreaths laid on behalf of EUOTC and the Royal British Legion Scotland. The service was attended by the Director Territorial Army, Major-General T. H. Birkbeck CB CBE DSO and Col J. S. Gratton OBE from the WO.

This was followed by a civic lunch in Otta and *'the rest of the day was spent drying clothing ... soaked by torrential rain during the ceremony'*.

On Monday morning, it was time to say farewell to Otta and head for Oslo; 110 Officers and Officer-Cadets travelled by train while the remainder drove in the Unit's vehicles.

The train party was in for a surprise, as Former WRAC Cadet Sergeant Fiona Heptonstall (MB ChB 1964 now Maclaren) explains:

> *We intended to get off the train in Lillehammer for an informal visit to the famous museum. To our consternation as the train drew in we found the platform lined with old service-men and -women proudly wearing their medals from the last war gathered to greet the soldiers from Scotland. Most of our officers had gone ahead to Oslo so a frantic 'O-Group' was held and it was decided that a gentle shamble up the hill was not in order. We formed up outside the station with the pipes and drums followed by the WRAC and then the men, making it a large contingent We had a march-past at the salute and then marched up to the museum. We had enormous fun in the OTC but on this occasion the importance of the work done by the Army in war and times of unrest came home to us and I only hope we showed them the respect they deserved. It was a very timely reminder to us of dark days in the past. The pipe band were in cracking form that day ...*

On arrival in Oslo, the Contingent formed up, dressed in kilts and marched through the streets of Oslo behind the Pipes & Drums to their billets at the Guards' Barracks. They had, of course, been well aware that Norwegian television and press had followed every stage of their progress and reported daily.

George Livingstone-Learmonth:

Perhaps the best thing about the March, was that being historic for Norway it was given a lot of publicity and we appeared on the front pages of the national and local press most days, and there was also a nightly spot on television reporting on our progress and filming as we always put on a good show when we marched into our town for the night. We paraded every evening, marched about with the pipes, stamped our feet with a bit of drill, and then generally were invited to a local celebratory banquet. Robin McKinley was a near-celebrity as he was usually in the front of the band and highly photogenic.

Despite this high profile, the cadets had not fully appreciated the level of interest it had stirred in Oslo and were surprised at the warmth of the welcome they received. The streets were lined with applauding onlookers and on arrival at the Barracks each officer and Officer-Cadet was presented with a booklet entitled 'Welcome to His Majesty the King's Guard and Oslo'. This gave a detailed schedule of ceremonial, sightseeing and social events for the duration of the visit.

After being formally welcomed by the Commander-in-Chief of His Majesty's Guards, the Contingent left for Akershus Castle where they paraded at the Norwegian War Memorial. This was followed by a march through the city to the University where Colonel Campbell presented a letter from the Principal of the University of Edinburgh to the Rector of Oslo University who then addressed the visitors.

The Pipes and Drums performed Beating Retreat before a large crowd in the University Square before leading the march to the City Hall. The CO presented a letter from the Lord Provost of Edinburgh to the Mayor of Oslo who also addressed the guests before hosting a civic reception, followed by a tour of City Hall.

In the evening, the Officer-Cadets were entertained by the students of the Oslo University Summer School.

Alasdair Geater recalls:

As I remember it, the highlight was a singsong by the OTC members, all Scottish songs such as 'The Bonnie Lass o' Fyvie-o', 'Macpherson's Rant', etc. As always at that time, the singing was led by George Fleming. He had a wonderful voice and an enormous repertoire of Scottish and Irish songs. He was slightly older than most of us as he had done National Service in the Argylls, and had earned a General Service Medal. He was the only cadet with a ribbon on his battledress blouse.

Wednesday and Thursday were spent sightseeing with knowledgeable guides including a boat trip on Oslo Fjord. Friday included a visit to the NATO Headquarters at Kolsas and in the evening the Pipes and Drums performed in the Band Stand in the centre of Oslo, followed by a reception hosted by the Caledonian Society of Norway. Also that evening, Norwegian television broadcast a 30-minute programme on Sinclair and the OTC's exploits.

Alasdair Geater describes another example of the warmth of the Norwegian welcome:

On morning parade one day shortly after the OTC arrived in the King's Guard barracks in Oslo, all cadets who came from North of Inverness were ordered to assemble separately. There were about half a dozen. They were introduced to an utterly charming Norwegian gentleman who turned out to be the son of Nansen, the famous explorer. He had come to Scotland when the Germans invaded Norway during World War II and had spent a lot of time in the North. He told us he wanted to repay the hospitality he had received there. Over the next few days, he took the group to visit the museum where his father's famous ship, the 'Fram', is preserved and entertained the members of the group in his home, at a restaurant and at the Royal Oslo Yacht Club. On the OTC's last day in Oslo, he came down to the docks to see them off. A most delightful person giving a wonderful display of Norwegian hospitality.

On Saturday morning, the Royal Guard presented the Unit with a bronze replica of the War Memorial which stands at the main entrance to their barracks and the rest of the day was free for rest and relaxation. George Livingstone-Learmonth explains:

> We had a day's initiative exercise to see what we could achieve (in army parlance) but more accurately in everyday language, to see what we could get up to. With one or two others I went to Denmark which we thought was a pretty good effort but no one was unduly impressed as most people had had a pretty good time and done something worthwhile.

The visit was rounded of with an evening cocktail party in Oslo harbour on HMS *Plover*, which had arrived on schedule.

The following morning the WRAC flew back to Edinburgh on a military aircraft as described by Fiona Maclaren:

> This plane was for troop carrying and had a bare fuselage with wooden benches down the sides so that we faced each other and a mechanism running down the centre of the roof to which parachutes [static-lines] could be attached! Regulations stated we must wear parachutes but no instructions were deemed necessary!

The men sailed from Oslo arriving in Rosyth on the 16th. Douglas Proudlock recalls:

> We came back on HMS Plover *which had subsequently been repaired. The return trip was notable for its stormy weather and folk going green at the gills.*

And George Livingstone-Learmonth:

> HMS Plover *was a Mine Layer. We slept in the stern which was open to the sea, between the rails down which the mines were moved on their way into the water, and we used the iron rails*

as pillows. For some of the time it was quite rough with the stern going up and down about 20 ft.

Despite the discomforts, their journey was somewhat more straightforward than that of one group of students who feared that the Navy might not get them back in time for graduation ceremonies. Alasdair Geater explains:

At the end of the time in Oslo, there were several of us who had to be back in Edinburgh for our graduation ceremonies. The RNVR had said during the planning phase of the whole operation that these cadets probably would get back on HMS Plover *in time but this could not be guaranteed. Alternative arrangements had, therefore, been worked out. We saw off the main body from Oslo docks and the following day were driven by the Norwegian Army to an air force base nearby. There we boarded a transport aircraft of the Norwegian Air Force, an American aircraft known as the 'Flying Boxcar'. Parachutes had to be worn throughout the flight. This necessitated removing our kilts and donning trousers. Fortunately, or perhaps not, no cadets from the WRAC section of the OTC were in the party. The aircraft set off for a Dutch military airbase near The Hague but the flight was briefly interrupted by an unscheduled landing at Schipol Airport, as fuel was apparently running low! We then had the rest of the day off to explore The Hague, one enterprising piper earning some beer money by busking in assorted cafés. An evening train then took us to the Hook of Holland for a ferry to Harwich. There, we entrained for London and then Edinburgh. To the amazement of all, the OTC Pipes and Drums were waiting on the platform at Waverley to welcome us home. The RNVR had delivered well on time.*

Within three weeks, the vehicles were back in Edinburgh and a semblance of normality had returned, but for all those who had taken part in SKOTTETOGET 1963 there was a feeling that somehow things had changed. David Bayne:

I would like to record my deep respect and admiration for the input of the WRAC. Their work was invaluable to those of us on the march. The did medivac, drove support trucks, set up camp-sites, etc and were a hugely important factor in helping to maintain morale. They even offered to clean spare kit and in the unlikely event of OCdt Eileen Winstanley reading this, I would like my spare shirt back.

It was quite a walk ... !

Chapter 7

Edinburgh & Heriot-Watt Universities' OTC

OVER THE NEXT few years, the normal training routine continued, with the Artillery and Engineer Sub-units attending Easter attachments at Larkhill and Chatham respectively while the Infantry, Signals and Pipe Band enjoyed a greater variety of locations. Annual camps continued to be for the whole Contingent, focusing on personal and leadership development, and the Pipe Band was regularly in the public eye including Beating Retreat on the esplanade at Edinburgh Castle each year. However, there were more changes to come.

Although the OTC WRAC Sub-units had been disbanded as recently as 1st October 1963, the WO wrote to Universities in March 1964 stating that female undergraduates would be permitted to join a local WRAC Unit with Officer Cadet status and train, including annual camp, with the OTC. They would be paid as privates in the WRAC and would not be liable for mobilisation with their parent Unit. The Edinburgh MEC felt that this was not practicable and, since the strength of the Edinburgh Contingent justified an additional Sub-unit, advised the OTC to apply for a WRAC Sub-unit. In the event, however, the WO plan was implemented successfully and 36 females were recruited at the start of the 1964/65 academic year.

In September 1965 a REME Sub-unit was re-established and an Officer Cadet earned a gallantry award. *The London Gazette* of 18th March 1966 carried the following report:

Beating Retreat at Edinburgh Castle, 1962.
Dairmid Lindsay

Piper's plaid brooch.
Dairmid Lindsay

King Olaf of Norway inspects the Guard of Honour at the University of Edinburgh Medical School, Edinburgh, 1962.

WRAC emplaning for Norway, 1963.

Fiona Maclaren

University of Edinburgh OTC on the march in Norway with one piper, 1963.

George Livingstone-Learmonth

Skottetoget, Andalsnes 1963.
Scott Lindsay

Pipes & Drums, in Skottetoget, Andalsnes 1963.
Scott Lindsay

Above and below:
Skottetoget marchers taking a break, Norway, 1963.

George Livingstone-Learmonth

'Mock' Edinburgh City Police Pipe Band, Grassmarket (above)
and Princes Street (below), 1966.

Diarmid Lindsay

Above: Honorary Colonel after
re-badging ceremony, Forrest Hill
Officers' Mess, 1976.

Julia Kneale

Below: RE Sub-unit building a
Bailey Bridge, 1977.

Julia Kneale

R.A.M.C. SONG.

This Song originated in the

EDINBURGH UNIVERSITY R.A.M.C.

(Volunteer and Officers'l Training Corps)

and has been a Popular Song in that Unit since 1885.

Tune—Varmer Giles.

NOW lads I'll endeavour to sing you a song,
With this blessed piano to help me along;
And as for the subject, why, what should it be,
But those jolly fine fellows, the R.A.M.C.

CHORUS:

Ri-tooral-ay-ooral-ay-ooral-ay-aye,
We follows the fighting line most of the day,
We picks up the wounded wherever they be,
We're jolly fine fellows, the R.A.M.C.

When you're chock full of bullets, and bung full of dints,
We wraps you and pads you and puts you in splints,
Then up on the knees of old 1, 2 and 3:
And you sends up a prayer for the R.A.M.C.

(Chorus).

Lift stretchers, the order, and then adjust slings,
We walks with our knees like the best sofa springs,
We gives you a drink, though it's only beef tea,
And then you thanks Heaven for the R.A.M.C.

(Chorus).

When your day's work is o'er, you goes out for some fun,
And you gets a sore head from the heat of the sun:
We gives you black draught and of No. 9's three,
And you calls down a curse on the R.A.M.C.

(Chorus).

When we sees these ere fighting chaps out with their guns,
Going flop on their bellies, and taking short runs,
We feels jolly thankful that they isn't we,
And we praises our luck in the R.A.M.C.

(Chorus).

The QUEEN has been graciously pleased to approve the award of the British Empire Medal for Gallantry (Military Division) to the undermentioned:

24006858 Officer Cadet Alan Sinclair ROBERTSON, Officers Training Corps.

On the evening of 25th September 1965, in complete darkness and heavy rain, an Army Vehicle driven by Officer Cadet Robertson of Edinburgh University O.T.C., became stranded at mid-stream whilst attempting to ford the River Tweed during a Territorial Army exercise.

The ford was in fact impassable in the existing conditions, but since neither he nor his team mates had any knowledge of the locality, they were unable to make a sound judgement of the situation and were indeed misled by seeing the rear lights of a vehicle moving up the opposite bank. The lights were those of a Recovery Vehicle attempting to tow out a previously stranded vehicle.

The river, which at this point was about 50 yards wide, and normally about 2 feet deep, had risen in violent flood to a depth of 4 to 6 feet and was a raging torrent. Officer Cadet Robertson and his crew managed to attract the attention of the recovery personnel on the far bank, who threw a rope, which after several attempts, was secured to the Vehicle. It was with the assistance of this rope that they were to attempt to reach the bank.

Officer Cadet Kariango, W.R.A.C. (T.A.), a non-swimmer, went first, but was swept down stream. Officer Cadet Robertson, realising her peril, struggled to the bank, and after running for some 100 yards, located her by her screams, dived into the torrent fully clad and finally got her to the bank.

His indomitable courage, perseverance and desperate effort in terrifying conditions undoubtedly saved Officer Cadet Kariango's life.

Officer Cadet Robertson received his medal at a ceremony in Edinburgh Castle attended by his CO and representatives of the University and MEC.

Astonishingly, in 1966 the WRAC Sub-units again came under threat of disbandment and various Universities, including Edinburgh, HQ Scottish Command and COMEC all lobbied vigorously for their retention. At the annual meeting of COMEC in September, the MOD gave assurances that the OTC would continue for at least one further year and would continue to recruit both men and women, but also announced that it was being evaluated on the basis of the number of Regular Officers produced The Army Board had set up a committee to study the interface between the Army and Higher Education and the intangible value was to be ignored because it was so difficult to assess.[32]

At the COMEC AGM the following year, the Director, Volunteers, Territorials and Cadets (DVT&C) reported that the committee reviewing the interface between the services and the Higher Education sector had not yet reached any conclusions. However, the Army had made known its view that the value of the OTC could not be ascertained in purely arithmetic terms and that, if it were *'abolished it would not be possible to resurrect it in our time'*.

The DVT&C then gave a brief report on the work of the committee and its thorough approach, noting that it was consulting widely and considering a full range of possible options. He hoped that the results would be published soon and did not think *'that his audience would be disappointed by them'*. There was again discussion on the concern that the primary role of OTCs should be recruitment of Regular officers; the university representatives were unanimous in the view that this was inappropriate and would have a seriously adverse effect.[33]

Meanwhile, as the Territorial Army had been restructured, becoming the Territorial and Army Volunteer Reserve, and reduced in size, some premises were surplus to requirements and the University of Edinburgh took the opportunity to purchase the Forrest Road Drill Hall.

Lt Col C. H. K. Corsar, who had recently assumed command felt that as Heriot-Watt had gained university status in 1965 and that a significant number of Officer Cadets were students at Heriot-Watt, the Unit's title (Edinburgh University OTC) was no longer appropriate. On 20th November 1967, he proposed a change to the MEC and it was decided to seek permission from the MOD to rename the Unit to The Edinburgh and Heriot-Watt Universities' Contingent of the Officers Training Corps. This was approved and the change took effect from 1st January 1968.

Also in 1968, individual overseas attachments were introduced whereby Officer Cadets could enjoy up to two weeks with a regular Army Unit overseas, usually alone but sometimes in small groups of two, three or occasionally four cadets. In the initial year, visits were made to Germany, Norway, Malta and Jamaica and over the next 20 years, Officer Cadets would add Libya, Gibraltar, Cyprus, Belize, Hong Kong, the Falkland Islands, South Georgia and even Hawaii to the list.

At the COMEC meeting in September 1968, the DVT&C announced that, despite the comments made by his predecessor the previous year, no decisions had yet been reached as regards the future of the OTC, observing that this *'brings home the slowness with which things move in Whitehall'*.[34]

The annual Remembrance Day Parade in Old College quadrangle was held in bitterly cold weather and it was decided that in future, the service would be held in the Playfair Library, followed by a parade and wreath-laying at the Memorial. This new format continues to this day.

The long-awaited review of the OTC and proposals for its future had finally been received and were considered by the CO and MEC to be reasonable. In a letter dated 15th January 1969, the MOD outlined the changes. Instead of having Sub-units for separate arms, each Contingent would be organised by type of training, namely into Basic, Advanced and Technical Wings. Although some smaller Contingents would have only the first two of these, Edinburgh and Heriot-Watt OTC would have all three. The change was brought into effect between 1st September 1969 and 31st March 1970. There would be savings in permanent staff but no change to establishment of Officer Cadets and TA officers.

The letter went on to acknowledge that the uncertainties of recent years had given rise to an *'unsettling effect'* on OTCs *'and it is the hope of the Army Board of the Defence Council that a more stable future lies ahead'.*

One unforeseen side-benefit of the change was perceived by the CO. As the Sub-units had disappeared so had their cap-badges; all Officer Cadets would now wear the same cap-badge and this would enhance loyalty to the Contingent instead of to the Sub-units. But there was a question mark over what that badge would be. Following the name change in 1968, the MEC had regularly discussed possible designs for a new badge but no decision had been reached.

The 1969 summer camp was at Benbecula. During the first week, the infantry carried out a joint exercise with Tayforth UOTC while the other Sub-units did specialist training. Former Engineer Officer Cadet Bill Simpson recalls:

> *The RE Sub-unit had a MACC task [Military Aid to the Civil Community] to build a wooden bridge – I don't recall if it was only a footbridge but I think it was. We travelled back and forward to the camp in 3-tonners for several days. There was a nearby village called 'Gramisdale' but quickly became known as 'Cramisdale' after the Sub-unit OC, Sandy Cram.*
>
> *We returned to the camp in the late afternoon. Mealtimes were rigidly adhered to and if you weren't there in time, you didn't eat. I recall one day we were a bit late on the way back so there was a general move to buy things from a local shop before we got back to camp. We spotted a shop on the way and the 3-tonner stopped to disgorge a load of tired and dirty cadets all clamouring to get served. The shopkeeper was an old fellow who was a bit overwhelmed and kept saying in a delightful island accent 'Och, take your time, take your time. The day is long'. It became a motto for the rest of the camp.*

During the second week the Contingent held an exercise based on Bonnie Prince Charlie's flight through the Hebrides after the defeat of his Jacobite supporters by the British Army at Culloden. A group of senior cadets played the part of the Prince and his entourage seeking to escape while the remainder of the Contingent tried to find and capture them. Bill Simpson continues:

It was really an exercise in infantry movement and control.

The Outer Hebrides are a string of islands with the main ones connected by roads built up over the water. Benbecula, which is small and flat, lies between North and South Uist which are long narrow islands running north–south. The exercise covered South Uist as well as Benbecula. The main north/south road runs down the western side of South Uist which also has a range of low hills.

It was decided to sweep down South Uist which is 20 miles long with one platoon on each side of the island and one on the central ridge. The platoon I was in was on the ridge which rises to roughly 2,000 feet. I was the radio operator and my recollection is that we used radios of Second World War vintage which were quite heavy; certainly pre-Clansman series. It was a struggle to get up the hills but on the top we found that the two platoons on either side couldn't communicate with each other because of the ridge so I had to relay messages from one to the other. It added interest to what was otherwise a pretty boring day – trudging along the top of the ridge.

At some point the weather turned very wet and cold and we had to don our gas capes to keep the rain at bay. We mostly ate 'compo' rations but in the evening got a hot meal which seemed to consist of some meat in a greasy gravy eaten in our mess tins at the side of the road. Under the circumstances it tasted wonderful!!!

During the dark hours, rest was taken and I did a spell on sentry duty. I remember trying to get some shelter behind a rock and as the sun came up, seeing another sentry a couple of hundred yards away silhouetted against the brightening sky. I recall thinking that in a real war situation, if he had been an enemy, I could have picked him off easily and he would have known nothing about it.

The bad weather continued and rather surprisingly, the powers that be decided to end the exercise on the second day (I

79

think). We were all cold and quite happy to get back to camp and a tot of 'grog'. The ablutions block contained a number of large, deep baths in wooden cubicles with open tops, tiled floors and cork boards on which to stand. The baths were unusually long and deep and there was no shortage of hot water. A number of us decided to have a 'steep' to warm up and it was one of the best feelings to lie absolutely flat with hot water up to my neck and luxuriate. One of the RE members was John Linehan also in our year for Civil Engineering. John came from the Borders and his party piece was to recite with appropriate inflections the however many verses there are of 'The Ballad of Eskimo Nell' a risqué poem in the style of 'The Shooting of Dan McGrew' by Robert Service.

He did this as we all lay in the baths and it is an abiding memory!!

'Bonnie Prince Charlie' got away!

In November the CO reported to the MEC that the three Wing system was working satisfactorily with the Wings named Infantry, Gunner and Engineer. The Infantry Wing included all first year Cadets and those taking Certificate B in Infantry. In their second year Officer-Cadets could remain in Infantry or move to the Gunner Wing for Royal Artillery or Royal Signals or to the Engineer Wing for Royal Engineers or REME.

The matter of accommodation again became an issue in 1972. The University Department of Machine Intelligence [later Artificial Intelligence], which occupied a small part of Forrest Hill, wanted to expand and had asked the University if the OTC could be relocated. The question was referred to the MEC who pointed out to the Professor concerned that, when the TA Association sold the property to the University, it was on condition that the University provided accommodation for the OTC. As there were no other suitable premises, it was politely but firmly suggested that the Department of Machine Intelligence find new premises.

In the autumn of 1972, the Army issued a statement on the new functions of the OTC. Including the following:

i)   The full designation will be 'The University Officers Training Corps'. Each contingent will be known by the title of its parent university or universities and student members will be designated 'officer cadets'.

ii) A Military Education Committee may recommend its parent university to withdraw recognition of a contingent and request the MOD to disband it, if it is considered that the maintenance of the contingent is not in the interests of the university.

iii) The role of the UOTC will be:

   a)   To provide a practical link between the Army and the universities thereby fostering interest in and under-standing of the Army and its role as an instrument of defence policy.

   b)   To provide training for undergraduates to prepare them for commissions in the Regular Army, TAVR and Cadet Forces.

   c)   To supervise, administer and train in accordance with current MOD instructions, University Cadets and Regular Army officers in residence at universities.

   d)   To inform, advise and assist undergraduates who are potential candidates for commissions in the Regular Army, TAVR and Cadet Forces.

In 1973, the MEC received a special report on MACC projects. The Engineer Wing had built a bridge in Benbecula, three in the Beinn Eighe Nature Reserve, with a fourth planned, and had done work at Firbush Point, a University recreation centre on the southern shore of Loch Tay. In the years ahead, they would build bridges at Cromdale, near Granton-on-Spey, at a nature trail near Strathyre, over the Alt Mhor in the Cairngorms, on Arran, near Irvine and in Glen Tanar.

For the first time, female Officer Cadets participated in the Scottish Country Dancing display in the Edinburgh Military Tattoo.

The Unit suffered another tragedy in September 1974 when Officer Cadet James Cooper was killed on an exercise in Germany.[35]

He joined the UOTC in March 1972 and attended a TAVR Parachute Course in May 1974. He intended to join 15th Scottish (V) Battalion Parachute Regiment after graduating and was attached to that Battalion for a NATO exercise in September when 554 paratroops were dropped from 36 Hercules aircraft in the region of the Kiel Canal. General Sir Mike Jackson, who also jumped that night, recalls:

> *Visibility. Excellent – a clear warm evening.*
> *Wind. The wind speeds at dropping height (800ft) and on the ground were very similar – around 6 knots directly on the nose. But unknown to the navigators there was a wind shear at around 4/500 ft with speeds of 15 knots plus. Thus the point of despatch/point of landing calculation was skewed with the early jumpers in each aircraft being despatched too close to the canal …*
> *It was a miserable night …*

Tragically, 15 men landed in the canal. German rescue boats were on hand for such an emergency and reacted well but six soldiers were drowned. After an inquiry it was reported to Parliament that three had apparently not attempted to inflate their life jackets and the other three life-jackets had failed to inflate because the CO_2 bottles were not screwed fully home. This led to revised procedures for the maintenance and issue of life jackets.

Representatives of the UOTC, MEC, the University and the Parachute Regiment attended James Cooper's funeral in Kirkcaldy and in May 1975, 15th Scottish (V) Battalion Parachute Regiment planted a memorial tree, a Norwegian Spruce, in the grounds of Pollock Halls, again attended by members of James Cooper's family and representatives of the UOTC and MEC.

The 1976 annual camp at Warcop, was shared with Cambridge UOTC. Apart from the usual friendly rivalry there was a fair amount of socialising as former Officer Cadet Mike Blair recalls:

They were invited to our mess, and one was heard to observe that they didn't have parties like that at Cambridge, to receive the reply 'Well you will on Thursday!' when we had a reciprocal invitation to their mess. In order to show off, it was decided to do a sixteen-some reel. This took a lot of practice, but despite the generous hospitality, we managed it with only one error ... and that was covered up.

Mike Blair also describes the social events enjoyed by the gunner Sub-unit at Otterburn, where they went three times per annum with Glasgow, Northumbria and Leeds UOTCs to fire 25-pounders.

I saw the well known competition where a cadet bet any challenger that he could drink a pint of beer with a teaspoon faster than the challenger could eat 3 Jacobs Cream Crackers without any liquid. The Beer man won ... just!

The next night, one of the band [a piper] climbed up onto the parapet wall running round the outside of his billet block at about midnight, and, having had a few beers, gave an impromptu rendition while walking unsteadily along the wall, some 10 feet above the ground. He was alternately urged on by his pals, and abused by the cadets who were trying to sleep. The Guard were not at all sure what to do, and the Orderly Officer – a 2Lt subaltern in his 4th year at University – was summoned. His exhortations had no effect to the music at all, and the situation was only resolved when the TA Cook WOII (whose name I forget) came out of his accommodation and in forthright terms said he had to get up to cook breakfast for 'the lot of you' at 0430 and to 'shut the **** up!' There was an immediate bagpipe deflating noise, and all was quiet.

From 6th to 11th July 1976, the British Forces staged a Scottish Military Tattoo at Wolf Trap Farm Park in Virginia as part of the United States Bicentennial celebrations.

Former Officer Cadet/Second Lieutenant Julia Kneale (BVM&S 1978) participated in the Scottish Country Dance team:

There were contingents from Aberdeen, Edinburgh and Heriot Watt, Glasgow and Strathclyde, and Tayforth UOTCs, and I was lucky enough to be chosen. We were selected and rehearsed within our Units then went to the Household Division barracks at Hounslow for group rehearsals before flying out to the USA. We were housed in the USMC Base at Quantico and treated with great hospitality.

We were issued with white tropical uniforms for the visit and danced in white dresses with tartan sashes.

A new cap and sporran badge design had been approved in 1975 and on Thursday 21st October 1976, HRH The Duke of Edinburgh, Honorary Colonel visited the Unit at Forrest Hill to present the new cap-badges to a representative party of Officer Cadets. The ceremony was followed by a reception in the Officers' Mess attended by the Principals of teh University of Edinburgh and Heriot-Watt University. Second Lieutenant Julia Kneale was present:

I told the Duke that I was considering joining the Royal Army Veterinary Corps and would be its first female member, to which his response was 'If I were you I'd burn my bra, blaze a trail and join them'. I partially followed his advice and was glad I did so as I ended up as a full Colonel with an OBE.

Around this time, Major David Bayne (who had participated in Skottetoget) was appointed Second-in-Command and Major Alistair Thom, a Regular, was Training Major and due to take over command in 1977. They decided that the matter of uniform needed to be considered.

Major Bayne recalls:

The change to trews came about because when I returned to the Unit in 1976 I noticed that while many of our young men were growing taller, they were not growing wider, and when they appeared on parade in kilts they looked like deck-chairs with awnings loosely draped over them. Totally independently Alis-

tair Thom (RHF) the Training Major and incoming colonel and a Regular, had formed the same opinion so we put our heads together and agreed:

- *the Regimental affiliation had always been with the Royal Scots;*

- *Royal Scots no longer had any kilted battalions;*

- *the kilt, while decorative, is hugely impractical;*

- *subjectively, trews would look smarter; and*

- *Hunting Stewart trews were in plentiful supply.*

There was initial resistance from the MEC and a sub-committee of the OTC was formed to consider the matter in depth. It supported the views of David Bayne (who replaced Lt Col Thom as CO on 1st January 1978) and the MEC agreed, despite the reluctance of the convener, Lord Balerno. In 1978 trews replaced the kilt although the Pipes and Drums continued to wear the kilt.

The RA Sub-unit narrowly avoided disbandment. For some time, it had been operating without a Permanent Staff Instructor. Vigorous efforts had been made to rectify the situation but without success and the CO felt that, since they were still equipped with obsolete 25-pounder Field Guns, the RA Section should be disbanded. The MEC initially agreed but early in 1979 the Unit was advised that it would receive a gunner PSI and the MEC retracted its decision. However, it would be another three years before the 25-pounders, which had served the Unit for over 30 years, were replaced by 105 mm Pack Howitzers.

In November, the UOTC suffered another loss when Captain Ailsa Ramsey, a former Officer Cadet and now the Officer Commanding the WRAC Unit, died in a parachuting accident.

David Bayne:

I recall the event. It was a weekend when the Sub-units were 'doing their own thing' and I was about to visit one in E. Loth-

ian when my wife phoned to say I should call in at home on the way. She had bought a copy of The Sunday Post *and it was on the front page. Ailsa was a keen member of the Perth & Kinross Free Fall Club and on that particular weekend she had decided to go there. Quite simply her parachute failed to open and eyewitnesses said that all the way down she could be seen to be trying to open the reserve chute, to no avail. It was simply one of those very sad 'one-in-a-million' accidents ...*

In December 1978, the Unit was re-organised into Basic, CMT and Advanced Training Companies. The structure was:

HQ Company:	Administration, CMT Training, Pipes and Drums
Infantry Company:	Basic Training for all and Advanced Infantry Training.
Support Company:	RA, RE, RSigs, REME/RCT.

David Bayne explains why he had decided the change was necessary:

I was about to take evening parade and all the officers were about to fall in when along sauntered this bright young gentleman sporting a shiny new pip on each shoulder and the brown beret of the Brigade of Guards. He wandered past us all, including the CO, without so much as a cheery wave and when I challenged him about saluting senior officers on parade was informed, totally seriously, that it was his impression that only Guards officers were to be saluted. He was very quickly put straight, but it seemed to me there was a need for basic training to be carried out. This would be carried out in the Infantry Company then the cadets would move to HQ Company for CMT training.

The Certificate of Military Training was at that time an essential for anyone hoping to apply for a commission and consisted of all the skills a platoon commander would be expected to possess. It consisted of Fieldcraft (movement, signals, map-

reading, etc.), administration, basic military law, methods of instruction and tactics. At Easter each year all the OTCs would gather at one of the universities and for one week the students were assessed on all of these skills culminating in a large-scale TEWT [Tactical Exercise Without Troops], *the whole thing being supervised by a staff Lt. Col.*

Having passed this the cadets would proceed to the Advanced Wing where they would do special-to-arm training in the Support Company or advanced infantry Training in the Infantry Company. At this stage they were encouraged to liaise as much as possible with local TA Units.

Chapter 8

'An Example
to Us All'

A TYPICAL OTC career at this time was described by 2/Lt Griselda Stevenson writing in a HWUOTC Newsletter published in October 1986:

I joined the OTC at the start of my first year at university, encouraged both by existing members and the thought of boosting my bank balance.

The first term was spent in recruit training which was hard work but great fun; learning basic military skills and simply beginning to understand a little of how the army works. In the Spring Term we began Sub-unit training, and for me it was the Infantry Sub-unit. For two terms we trained together, building up a Sub-unit spirit and the culmination of this training was two weeks of Annual Camp held at the end of the Summer Term.

Second year was dominated by the Certificate of Military Training, now replaced by MTQ2. CMT took the form of a term's training, a week's intensive course, and then a series of examinations. Following that course, I went on a fortnight's attachment to Germany where I visited HQ BAOR.

The following Autumn I was fortunate enough to spend another 3 weeks in Germany, taking part in Exercise Lionheart, where I was involved in looking after visitors. This gave me a wonderful opportunity to travel round many locations. I was abroad again the following Easter, this time for a fortnight in Cyprus on attachment with the WRAC.

During my third and fourth years I was involved in the organization and training of second year cadets. By this stage I wanted to continue in the TA after university and so started the process of 'going for a commission'. This meant sitting before two selection boards and then going to Sandhurst for a fortnight this past summer. This process took four years but some Officer Cadets can gain their commissions after three years.

At the COMEC meeting in September 1983, the Director, Territorial Army and Cadets (DTAC) presented a paper laying out a number of perceived problems with the UOTCs. It noted that only around 6% of Officer Cadets took TA commissions and half that number Regular Commissions. The tone of the presentation was felt to be unduly negative and the Secretary of COMEC sought clarification. The DTAC responded in detail explaining that the paper had indeed focussed on the problems in order to highlight them and the value of the UOTCs was not in question, merely the possibility of improvements to the mutual benefit of both UOTCs and the TA.

The essence of the seven issues is worth noting as they would lead to significant changes.

1) The Title. Many in the Regular Army (which in 1980 had a lower proportion of former OTC members than is the case today) thought the OTC was *'something to do with the Cadet Force rather than the TA'*. A change of title (University Volunteers (TA) was offered as a possibility) would do much to improve the image as well as better reflecting the reality that most members were not going to become officers.

2) The Military Role (or lack of one). The UOTCs were not liable to call-out on mobilisation. This lack of a war role meant that UOTC units had a lower priority for manning and equipment than the rest of the TA.

3) Regular Manning. The relatively low priority given to manning the Regular staff posts in UOTCs, an increasing shortage of captains and majors and a widely-held view that a UOTC appointment for a Regular officer was unattractive,

combined to make it unlikely that the staffing difficulties would ease. The DTAC felt that a specific military role could improve both the image and the manpower situation.

4) Contact with the wider TA. UOTCs tended to be insular. This was understandable given the nature of university life but meant that the UOTCs did not attract young TA officers. Furthermore, Officer Cadets tended to regard the UOTC as part of their university rather than the TA and leave both when they graduated.

5) Shortage of TA Officers. Generally, TA officers were not at-tracted to the OTC, preferring the challenge of a TA unit with a war role. The traditional source of OTC officers, the university staff, was not providing enough volunteers and yet the need was great as Units typically had only one Regular officer, either the CO or the Training Major.

6) Lack of a Specific Training Aim. It was felt inappropriate to have the UOTC focus wholly on officer training, since two-thirds of members would not become officers. This was under review. [In a sense, this is a repetition of the view ex-pressed in 1946 when the priority was changed from Certifi-cate B training to 'leadership development'.]

7) Organisation of UOTC Training. Units varied widely in terms of number and range of Sub-units with some having none and the largest having seven. There was no discernable difference in morale, enthusiasm, attendance or recruitment in the different types of Unit but there was a significant ad-ditional cost in having Sub-units. The same training could be achieved more cheaply through courses and attachments to Regular and TA Units.

A number of options and solutions were offered, notably the possibility that UOTCs assume responsibility for training officers for the TA as a whole. COMEC and MECs were invited to develop a coordinated response by the end of March.

Seventeen MECs responded to COMEC and a detailed letter

was sent to DTAC on 4th April, noting *inter alia* the unanimous view of MECs that there should be no name change and that relations with the rest of the TA were sound. The whole matter appeared to fade away quietly, but it was a temporary lull.

At the start of the autumn term in 1984, a new training syllabus was introduced. While not a consequence of the above, equally it was not unrelated. Instead of the Recruits Course followed by training for the Certificate in Military Training, cadets would henceforth seek to obtain the Military Training Qualification which was in two parts. They would train for MTQ1 in their first year, MTQ2 in second year and then concentrate on Special-to-arm.

MTQ1 consisted of the following elements: Workplace Induction, Leadership, Military Knowledge, Skill at Arms (Annual Personal Weapon Test), Fieldcraft and Tactics, Communication Skills, Map Reading, First Aid/Health and Hygiene, Fitness Training, Drill.

MTQ2 sought to build on MTQ1 and focused on leadership and management skills relevant to junior officers and included the 'seven questions estimate' or assessment of a situation or task, the orders process, more advanced map-reading, signals and public-speaking.

This change in training syllabus was soon followed by an updated Charter setting out the status (Group B of the TA), role and regulations. The role was:

1) *To provide a practical link between the Army and the Universities thereby fostering an interest in, and understanding of, the Army and its role as an instrument of defence policy.*

2) *To inform, advise and assist undergraduates who are potential candidates for commissions in the Regular Army, TA and Cadet Forces*

3) *To provide training for undergraduates to prepare them for commissions in the Regular Army, TA and Cadet Forces.*

4) To supervise, administer and train, in accordance with current MOD instructions, Undergraduate Cadets and Regular Army Officers in residence at Universities.

In 1986 the Unit's Pipes & Drums played at the opening and closing ceremonies of the Commonwealth Games in Edinburgh and a Scottish Country Dance team participated in the British Berlin Tattoo.

In 1987, the Berlin visit was repeated and the Unit won the Northern Lights competition, a feat repeated in each of the two following years.

In 1988, Colonel F. F. Gibb CBE, late Royal Scots, conducted an extensive and thorough review of the Corps. His insightful, logically argued and clearly presented report, was issued on 1st July and must have contributed significantly to the fact that the Corps' existence was not threatened over the next two decades.

The aim of the review was to *'examine the charter, organisation, administration, establishment and activities of the UOTC'.*

The scope was:

The future of the UOTC as a concept is not in doubt. However, in a climate of diminishing resources it is essential to optimise those devoted to the UOTC to the maximum benefit of the Army, consistent with harmonious coexistence with, and the needs of, the Universities.

In his Foreword, Col Gibb admitted that the study was an eye-opener and it is perhaps the case that this 'up-front' assertion was intended to condition his audience, which he undoubtedly knew to include a significant proportion of sceptics, to be prepared to be similarly enlightened:

I have found this study into the University Officers Training Corps a most rich and rewarding task as it confirmed all that is good in the young of today. For one, and I do not believe that I am alone in this respect, who had little or no conception of the role or function of the Corps, or the value it has not only to the Army in terms of the quality and quantity of officers it produces, but also to the country at large, this was an enlightening experience. For here is a group of young men and women who have a real sense of commitment, self-motivation and a keen desire to experience leadership and the military way of life. Frankly, they are an example to us all.

The Army has a privileged position in the Universities which is the envy of many Institutions, Banks, Commerce and Professions. It is one which we need to nurture and cherish because the future of the Officer Corps lies in the University Officers Training Corps.

The report notes that the UOTC Contingents were established before the expansion of tertiary education and that consequently there was '*no balance between the size or location of UOTCs and the undergraduate population* [of the] *catchment areas they cover*'. It was felt, however that there was little scope to redress the situation. A more manageable problem was a lack of standardisation in organisation and training in individual Contingents:

Individually, UOTCs are in a healthy state. Collectively they are a muddle. The objective must be to rationalise the latter without affecting the former ... . The case for producing a standard organisation with common training objectives is overwhelming.

The report identified clear values of the Corps to the country, the universities, the Officer Cadets themselves and to the Army, noting *inter alia* that: '*Twice this Century, the UOTC has provided the mainstay for the Officer Corps in time of need*'.

On the matter of recruitment of officers for both the Regular and Territorial Army, it was recognised that increasingly these would come from the Higher Education sector and the Review Team initially proposed to raise the profile of 'recruitment'. As the review progressed, however, and in particular as they consulted

MECs, they quickly recognised that any such moves would not be welcome and, in any case, could prove to be counter-productive. Their conclusions were that the UOTCs must not be, or even be seen to be, recruiting organisations and instead should seek to give Cadets a rewarding and enjoyable experience and trust that this would attract a sufficient number to the Army way of life.

Detailed recommendations were made as regards training and organisation and special consideration was given to female Officer Cadets. While recommending no change to the existing policy of re-cruiting (into the UOTC) 30% females it concluded that there was:

> ... an urgent need to reappraise the employment of female offi-cers in the Regular and Territorial Army ... . Greater employ-ment of female officers may be the only solution to maintaining the quality of the Officer Corps.

It was also recommended that female Officer Cadets should wear the UOTC cap-badge instead of that of the WRAC; this would be the final step in full integration of female cadets.

Two changes to the OTC Charter were recommended. Firstly, the four elements of the role should be prefaced 'There are four equal aims of the OTC' to eliminate a widely-held view that the first-stated role (providing a practical link between the Army and the Universities) was its principal purpose. Secondly, insert the word 'encourage' in the second aim ('inform, assist and encourage undergraduates who are potential candidates for commissions'). In this context, potential candidates meant Officer Cadets who had already indicated a possible interest in taking a commission. 'En-couraging' them was therefore not inconsistent with the policy of no recruitment.

In 1989, Lt Col Ron Abbott, a Regular officer of the Royal Sig-nals, took over command from Lt Col Bill Percy. Hitherto, the CO had almost always been a TA officer, supported by a Regular Train-ing Major but henceforth both appointments would alternate be-tween Regular and TA such that a TA CO was supported by a Regular Training Major and vice versa.

Although there had been a time when an OTC appointment was generally seen as unhelpful to a Regular officer's career progression, this was changing and Ron Abbot enjoyed his spell in Edinburgh. He outlines some highlights of his three years with the Unit:

It was a delight to meet a lot of very well motivated and intelligent young people of both sexes who, even though they represented the best educated 20% of the population, were a pleasure to work with. Many of them went on to make very good Army officers whom I have met subsequently: they are now of the rank of Lt Col or higher.

However, the training programmes had to be very carefully planned as the audience was pretty critical if it was not, and this was done with limited resources and by calling in favours from the contacts that you had around the place.

In 1990, we also managed to take the Officer Cadets for their first overseas camp since 1963. It was only to Germany – Hohne – but it was very successful and enjoyed by all.

I also managed to obtain authority to recruit Officer Cadets from a Commonwealth country – Barbados – and in doing so had the TA Regulations changed to accommodate this. It is interesting to see that the Regular Army continues to recruit many from the Commonwealth.

A particularly fond memory was seeing the OTC shooting-team beat the Glencorse Instructors' Team from Glencorse Training Organisation in a Falling Plate competition. We had the old SLR and the instructors had the new SA80 – they were really fed up at being beaten by students! However, we had a very good PSI shooting coach and we were able to obtain plenty of ammunition for practice in those days.

I also recall that we won the inter-Scottish Universities Northern Lights competition which included our Scottish Country Dancing Team beating the Glasgow University Team who had appeared on TV and really thought they would sweep the board!

Major Tom Buchanan, a Regular Royal Scot, took over as Adjutant in February 1990:

My first big duty was to complete the organisation and arrangements for the Unit's summer camp which had been started by the CO and Major Al Prewer. This was to take place in Fallingbostel, West Germany in early July. Major Prewer had arranged for the camp to be based with one of his former Units – 40 Field Regiment RA. The movement of the Unit was to be in two parts – a road party consisting of the vehicles which were to be driven by the TA Permanent Staff and an air party for the remainder. Both parties travelled to and from BAOR with no major hiccups. An enjoyable two weeks was had training with the Regular troops and culminated in a three-day exercise on Soltau Training Area where the Unit was visited by the TA Scotland Commander who was visiting all TA Units in BAOR.

Former Officer Cadet Jim Fraser (BSc 1992) was at this camp:

We were hosted for the duration of the camp by what were at the time 40 Field Regiment Royal Artillery, also known as the Lowland Gunners, and hence there was very much a Scottish connection to the whole event, despite being on the edge of the Soltau Training Area.

The training was of a type and scale that couldn't be imagined in the UK at the time and all of the students learned a lot more about armoured and defensive warfare than we ever had before. The facilities available both on the camp at Hohne and on the surrounding training area were a real eye opener for a bunch of university and college students. But there is a lot of history to the base at Hohne as well, particularly its proximity to the former Nazi camp at Bergen-Belsen. Although a formal visit to the memorial site wasn't included as part of the training programme, we were shown footage of the liberation of Bergen-Belsen. In fact as part of an orienteering exercise on the land surrounding Hohne, some of us stumbled upon the perimeter fence of the Bergen-Belsen memorial park and saw first-hand the size and scale of the tombs. It was a very sobering experience to see the numbers involved inscribed on one mound after another after another ...

Whilst we didn't have a pipe band for the Annual Camp, we did have a solo piper, Alan Graham, who was very much an active participant in the military side of the training. Both he and the Country Dancing team, of which I was a member, performed across a number of messes on the base. We were used to great effect to increase the profile of the OTC and also to emphasise the fact that the OTC wasn't just about military skills – there were some social skills involved too!

Many lasting friendships were made as a result of this interaction with our hosts, some of which are still going strong in 2014. One of my friends married one of the FOOs [Forward Observation Officer] from 40 Field for example!

On return from Annual Camp in BAOR the Royal Engineer's Troop performed a MACC task by building an Obstacle Course and 'Trim Trail' for Queen Victoria School, Dunblane. Over the next few years they would renovate the burial island of the McLeod Chieftains and construct a new bridge to the island, upgrade a footbridge at Tounge in Sutherland to one capable of taking a Land Rover and build a path and footbridge on the outskirts of Callander.

The next year, 1991, was relatively routine. The gunners fired two Royal Salutes from the Castle, the normal one for the Honorary Colonel's birthday and also one for the Queen Mother's Birthday as 105 Regt RA was unable to do so due to other commitments.

Several significant changes were initiated in 1992. The first was a decision to move from the Forrest Hill Drill Hall close to Old College in central Edinburgh to Redford Barracks on the western outskirts of town. The University had honoured its obligation to provide premises for the UOTC but it was no secret that the accommodation occupied could be put to good academic use. However, there were other reasons to move as Ron Abbott explains:

> *Regarding the move to Redford Barracks, I put this in place*
> *with rather mixed feelings. The Forest Hill TA Centre was very*
> *handy for bringing in the students from the University and I*
> *found that I had a great deal of close ties with Edinburgh Uni-*
> *versity at that time. I'd had some very interesting visits to what*
> *was then the Artificial Intelligence Faculty of the University who*
> *shared the building with us. However, it just was not practical*
> *or secure for an OTC which had to keep a lot of stores, includ-*
> *ing weapons, on the premises. There were frequent robberies*
> *and break-ins to the building. Although most of this was aimed*
> *at the computers in the AI Faculty, we were unable to separate*
> *our areas away from the faculty offices. The TAVRA at that*
> *time could not afford the works required to secure and maintain*
> *that TA Centre, so I looked elsewhere for a solution. It was at*
> *that time that the Yeomanry Regt and 15 Para Regt were re-or-*
> *ganised and thereby freed up space in the present home of the*
> *TA. This was also better placed for recruiting in many ways,*
> *because it was nearer to Heriot Watt and also very close to what*
> *had become Napier University. Most of the OTC recruits in my*
> *time came from Edinburgh and Napier. We had very few mem-*
> *bers from Heriot Watt: their campus was further out and even*
> *though we tried several times to improve recruiting there, the*
> *people who joined found travelling into the city to Forrest Hill*
> *too much of a strain on their studies.*

The post of Adjutant was changed from a Regular appointment to a Permanent Administration Staff Officer (PASO) post and Tom Buchanan was replaced by Captain Charles Inness, a recently re-tired Regular RA Major. As Tom Buchanan was due to retire from the Army the following year, he remained with the UOTC:

> *I then moved and worked exclusively from the new base loca-*
> *tion in Redford Barracks complex, liaising with the outgoing*
> *Units, the civil contractor and the Defence Lands Office. A few*

problems were encountered – mainly due to the new locations
of the outgoing Units not being available on the due dates, but
these were overcome and the work of converting the Drill Hall
to meet the needs of the OTC proceeded satisfactorily.

The second change related to the Unit's title. In June 1992, Napier Polytechnic acquired university status and, as a significant number of Officer Cadets came from Napier, it was decided that the current title of Edinburgh and Heriot-Watt Universities' OTC was no longer appropriate. Agreement was reached with the MEC to seek approval for the Unit's name to be changed to City of Edinburgh Universities' OTC and formal application was made to the MOD.

In 1993, the Unit was issued with, and converted to, the 5.56 mm SA80 Rifle, replacing the old SLRs, and in May hosted the Annual Northern Lights competition and were again overall winners. The major events of the year, however, were in September.

By the start of the new training year, agreement to the proposed name change had been obtained from the Honorary Colonel, HQ Scotland and HQ UKLF. Although formal approval was still awaited from the MOD the Unit adopted the new title with effect from the start of the new term.

Also in September, work on the new premises in Colinton Road was completed and the Unit transferred from Forrest Hill, the move being completed on the 23rd. The new facility was felt by all concerned to be first-class but there were fears that its location, far from the centre of the city, would adversely affect recruitment and attendance. These were to prove unfounded and applications continued to exceed the establishment of 167 Officer Cadets.

The Honorary Colonel visited the Unit on 2nd June, 1994, when he was welcomed by the Lord Provost, the Deputy Honorary Colonel and the Commanding Officer. After inspecting a Guard of Honour provided by two Gun Detachments of the RA Sub-unit, the Honorary Colonel gave a short speech and formally named the centre 'Duke of Edinburgh House'.

It was the start of a new era.

Chapter 9

Full
Circle

AT THE ANNUAL COMEC meeting in September 1994, it was announced that the MOD was again considering the use of UOTCs as the main training facility for officers for the Territorial Army. The Edinburgh MEC felt that this was likely to be a distraction and would strain resources which were already stretched due to financial constraints. The CO, however, felt that, at least in the short term, it was unlikely to be a major burden as there were adequate training resources for TA officers in Scotland and he foresaw little demand to use the OTC. This view was shared by HQ Scotland who responded to HQ UK Land Forces (UKLF) making the point that, while the OTCs felt that it would be feasible for them to undertake the second phase of TA Officer Training, the existing system in Scotland was running efficiently, did not involve the OTCs and should be retained. That was the end of the debate, at least for the time being.

The training pattern at this time was Special-to-arm training in the second term (supplemented by visits to Corps HQs), contingent adventure training at the Easter holiday and a contingent annual camp where the emphasis was on infantry skills and leadership training with a full social programme.

In 1995 the RE Sub-unit undertook a ten-day MACC project at Mugdock Country Park in Glasgow where they repaired paths, constructed a viewing area with disabled access and rebuilt the children's playing area. In 1997, they provided support to Historic Scotland and the University of Edinburgh at Finlaggan Loch on Islay. An archaeological dig was planned at a site which was normally under water and the engineers constructed a coffer dam, pumped the water out and helped with the excavations.

March 1996 saw the end of an era. General Sir Charles Guthrie, Chief of the General Staff, visited the Unit and later wrote to the CO, Lt Col Ian Hamilton, thanking him for the visit. In the letter Sir Charles commented:

> *It was a real privilege, too, to be able to make the presentation* [a pewter plate engraved with the details of his extraordinary service] *to Mr Peter Edwards. His is a wonderful story of dedication and service, and I was delighted to be able to mark his 'retirement' in this way.*

Peter Edwards, universally and affectionately known as 'auld Pete', had served the army in various capacities for some 60 years. He joined the Royal Artillery around 1936 aged 18, went to France with the British Expeditionary Force in September 1939 and was evacuated from Dunkirk. He served throughout the war becoming a Battery Sergeant Major. He continued to serve as a Regular until the late 1950s when he retired from the Army and joined Edinburgh OTC. David Bayne recalls:

> *Pete was a real character. He had been evacuated at Dunkirk and was a BSM later in the War and had a wonderful fund of stories. He also survived a court-martial where he was successfully defended by an Artillery officer named Charles Campbell, later CO, EUOTC. I never found out the reason for the court-martial. When I joined in 1960 he was the clothing storeman, cook, bottle-washer and general factotum.*

Alexander McCall Smith (LLB 1971) knew him ten years later:

> *Peter Edwards was the Quartermaster. Not only did his stores have all sorts of kit, but he was in charge of cooking when we went off on camp. Peter was allocated a certain sum of money per head and managed to cater magnificently with that, producing fantastic fried food, baked beans and such things that he la-*

dled into our rectangular mess tins. He also brewed large urns of tea. That tea had a particular flavour that I have never again encountered anywhere in the world. I feel quite nostalgic at the thought of it.

David Bayne continues:

When I went back as 2i/c in 1976, Pete was being discharged from the army because of his age, a mere 58. Because the OTC was his life, the then CO, Alistair Thom kept him on in an unofficial capacity as did I when I took over, paying him (at summer camp) out of our own pockets. He was one of those people every unit would love to have, someone who did all the jobs people preferred to leave to other people.

Pete continued working at the OTC voluntarily for another 20 years when age forced him to give it up. He passed away a few years later.

The RA Sub-unit continued to fire a 21-gun Salute each year on the Honorary Colonel's birthday and, in May 1997 also fired one to mark the opening of the General Assembly of the Church of Scotland. That year also saw them win the King George VI Cup in the annual inter-UOTC artillery competition, the first Scottish unit to do so.

By May 1997, establishment was down to 149 Officer Cadets but the Unit was authorised to recruit to 200. However the CO feared that a forthcoming Defence review would lead to a 20% reduction in training budget with a consequent further reduction in establishment, possibly to as low as 100 Cadets. This despite the fact that the Unit provided a steady steam of applicants for Regular commissions; 15 former members of the Unit completed the Sandhurst course in the summer and a further four had taken TA commissions.

In October 1997, Army Headquarters Scotland initiated a study into the four UOTCs under its command: Aberdeen, Edinburgh, Glasgow & Strathclyde and Tayforth. The GOC wrote to

MECs explaining that '*This is not a cost-cutting exercise. ... The UOTC is a splendid organization but cannot be allowed to lead a charmed life, especially when everything else is being looked at critically.*'

The resulting report was produced in May 1998 and included an assessment of OTC output in 1996/97. The statistics for CEUOTC showed that during the year there were 196 Officer Cadets in training, nine former members had graduated from Sandhurst and 19 members had passed the Regular and five the Territorial Commissions Boards. MTQ1 pass rate was 87% and MTQ2 83%. These figures were generally better than the other Scottish Universities and the range of results was seen as confirmation of the '*long-standing suspicion*' that there were inconsistencies in training between the Units, a point that had been emphasised in Col Gibb's review a decade previously!

Intangible outputs were assessed including the value to individuals such as leadership, self-reliance, team-working, organisational ability and communication skills. The Army recognised that the UOTCs provided it with privileged access to the student body, helped to maintain the profile of the Army through MACC tasks and ensured a stream of '*highly intelligent and positive members of society who can champion the cause of the Armed Forces*'. It was also perceived that the Universities gained through improved employability of members and the '*visibility*' of their OTCs through, for example, participation in the Edinburgh Military Tattoo and MACC projects. Society, too, benefited from the many former cadets who constituted a widespread body of informed opinion on military matters as well as the involvement of UOTC members in community-based projects, charity work and youth support activities. Many of the observations were a repetition of points made by Col Gibb in 1988.

One important point that had not been made previously was that while the number of students in tertiary education had mushroomed, UOTC manpower establishments had remained virtually static such that the proportion of students able to avail themselves of UOTC training was now tiny.

The report was very favourable to the UOTCs whose value was certainly not underestimated, and concluded that there were '*no significant efficiencies*' to be made. However, it identified inconsistencies between UKLF's training directive and the OTC Charter which should be corrected. Interestingly, it also invited UKLF to '*consider a structured expansion of OTCs to match the growth of tertiary education*'. That was not to eventuate; the OTC establishment was geared to the diminishing size of the Army rather than that of the expanding universities.

Meanwhile, during the Easter holiday, the RE Troop undertook training in the Netherlands as guests of 11 Engineer Battalion, Royal Netherlands Army, a visit described by the RSM as the best thing he had done in his army career. After annual camp at Barry Buddon, the Troop undertook more work on Islay, this time supported by Dutch sappers on a reciprocal visit.

The following three years were particularly eventful. In the autumn of 1998, the Unit received extensive media coverage when it provided the guard at Edinburgh Castle, the first time that females had performed the role. In May of the following year, the Unit was again successful in the Northern Lights competition, winning the drill, military skills, men's rugby and dancing contests, the overall Sports Cup and the Northern Lights Trophy. Some of the opposing rugby sides felt that CEUOTC had enjoyed an unfair advantage; five of their team played for the Army in Scotland!

As had been mentioned in the 1998 report on the Scottish UOTCs, many Officer Cadets undertook charity work and the like. Sadly, these efforts, while well-known in a general sense, are unrecorded, but it was reported to the MEC that, in the summer of 1999, six Officer Cadets cycled from Lands End to John O' Groats, raising £3,000 for charity.

The Honorary Colonel, The Duke of Edinburgh, attended the Haldane Dinner on 18th February, 2000 and gave a short address. Also present was Sir Malcolm Rifkind, the recently appointed Deputy Honorary Colonel.

During the training year 2000–01 a total of 22 former Officer Cadets entered Sandhurst. One CO felt that the '*very satisfactory*' numbers applying for Regular commissions was partly a consequence of *'the example set by the Permanent Staff Instructors, the standard of their instruction and their general enthusiasm'*. The deliberate policy of making the training interesting and enjoyable undoubtedly also played a part and it is interesting to note the full training and exercise programme for 2000–01 as an illustration of the activities available.

December
– 14 Officer Cadets participated in a skiing trip   Val d'Iserre

January/February
– Weapons weekend at Warcop: General Purpose Machine
   Gun, Light Support Weapon and Plastic explosives
– 18 Officer Cadets visited 19 Regiment RA   Colchester
– FIBUA [Fighting In Built Up Areas] weekend   Whinney Hill
– Two skiing weekends   Aviemore
– REME inter-UOTC competition   Bordon

March
– MTQ1 testing   Castlelaw
– RE Inter-UOTC competition   Minley
– Unit shooting weekend   Barry-Buddon
– Ex UTOPIAN VAGABOND (Cavalry)   Bovington
– Ex BRIEF ENCOUNTER (Artillery)   Larkhill
– Ex LIGHTNING STRIKE (Signals competition)   Blandford

April
– Skiing Expedition   France
– Ex NORTHERN LIGHTS competition   Cultybraggan

May
– ASSAM (Shooting Competition)   Barry-Buddon
– NATO Reserve Officers Shoot   Castlelaw

June
- Royal Gun Salute   Edinburgh Castle
- ANNUAL CAMP   Knook
    (including a three-day battlefield tour to YPRES)

July
- RE Bridge Building Camp   Luss, Loch Lomond
- King George VI Artillery Competition   Warcop
- Overseas Adventure Training   Canada

With such a range of pursuits on offer, it is little surprise that the Unit was flourishing: in 2002–03 strength was 293 Officer Cadets (including 36 Army bursars).

In the summer of 2003, following annual camp at Ripon, which was visited by the Honorary Colonel, a group of Officer Cadets embarked on a six-week expedition to Malawi, organised by themselves. After four weeks of mountaineering, kayaking and sub-aqua training they provided assistance to villagers building a new school.

At the start of the 2003–04 training year, the new CO, Lt Col Ewart Baxter introduced a revised structure of three training companies and a training support wing. Haldane Company provided the training for MTQ1, Christison Company for MTQ2 and Geddes Company for Advanced and Special-to-Arm.

Early in 2004, HRH The Duke of Edinburgh was appointed Royal Honorary Colonel and Sir Malcolm Rifkind became Honorary Colonel. These changes came as a surprise and not only to the Unit, as Sir Malcolm explains:

When I was first appointed, Prince Philip was Honorary Colonel and I was Deputy Honorary Colonel. That changed in 2004 when the MOD decided that he was to become Royal Honorary Colonel and I Honorary Colonel. Neither Prince Philip nor I was consulted on this change which was discourteous to say the least. The MOD asked me to inform Prince Philip of the change. When I did so, he replied that he was curious as to why they

*could not have informed him directly and he also wondered why
the word 'Honorary' had to be retained in his title. I think he
was right on both counts!*

In February 2008, the Centenary year of the OTC, HRH The
Duke of Edinburgh attended the Haldane Dinner and gave a short
address saying how impressed he always was when he visited the
Unit at camp and how much he admired the OTC in general and
CEUOTC in particular. He went on to say that he was the Honorary Colonel of several regiments but had recently been invited to
accept an appointment as Honorary Captain of a Unit and supposed he would soon be an Honorary Lieutenant! The Honorary
Colonel was also present and recalls:

*On the 100th Anniversary of the OTCs, the Royal Honorary
Colonel was invited to the annual Haldane Dinner and to our
delight he accepted. On the day he had himself flown up from
London, attended the dinner in full Mess dress and then late at
night was flown back to London. Sitting next to him at the dinner I mentioned to him that I understood he was flying back at
the end of the evening rather than staying the night. He confirmed that was the case. I confess I was surprised as he must
have been 89 at the time and such a day must have been very tir-
ing. I remarked, light-heartedly, that I supposed he preferred to
sleep in his own bed each night. He firmly put me in my place by
reminding me that he could have slept in his own bed in Edinburgh as well (meaning Holyrood Palace)!'*

That autumn, the MTQ was replaced by the Military Leadership Development Programme (MLDP) although the syllabus was
broadly similar to the MTQ. MLDP1 was basic training to enable
the new recruit to function as a soldier: subjects included drill,
map-reading, weapon handling, shooting, first aid and fieldcraft.
MLDP2 focused more on leadership, such as planning, developing
and issuing orders, and personal skills such as public speaking,
presentations and team work. The transition was straightforward

and 50 Officer Cadets passed MLDP in its first year and 232 in its second.

In 2009 the Adjutant General initiated a 'root and branch' review of the OTC '... *to identify how to improve the partnership with universities while increasing the OTC's outputs and effects in order to improve value for money'.* It would also examine '*the Army interface with the undergraduate population to determine how it might be improved and to make recommendations as to the future role and organisation of the 19 UOTCs'.* It would be two years before the study was completed.

Meanwhile, the nation was in a serious financial downturn, retrenchment was the order of the day and public spending was sharply curtailed. The MOD budget was reduced and savings simply had to be achieved. With ongoing operations in Afghanistan, the scope for flexibility was limited and the MOD took one of the few options open to it in the short term. The Territorial Army suffered swingeing cuts in activity, including restrictions on the use of TA Permanent Staff in UOTCs, and, much to the alarm of MECs and many others, Officer Cadet pay was suspended.

Despite this, recruitment in autumn 2009 was satisfactory and establishment (reduced to 138 a year previously) was again exceeded. Funding was restored in April 2010. Thanks to the officers' leadership and the enthusiasm of a solid core of Officer Cadets, the Unit survived the period of austerity but sadly fourteen cadets felt forced to resign in order to undertake paid employment.

The funding constraints had other consequences. In May 2011 the CO, Lt Col Doug McKay RA, a Regular who had steered the Unit through the worst of the crisis, reported to the MEC that there would be no MACC task that year and no more firing of Royal Salutes.

The team who had carried out the Review of the OTC produced their report in 2011. Several important recommendations were implemented almost immediately while others were to be trialled.

Notably, with effect from January 2012, all UOTC Contingents became part of the Royal Military Academy Sandhurst Group reporting ultimately to the Commandant RMAS, although individual UOTCs retained their titles, uniforms and badges. UOTCs became responsible for all Phase I training of Army Reserve Potential Officers. To this end, the training syllabus was updated and standardised around the Army Reserve officer commissioning programme and, as this was infantry-based training, all Special-to-Arm wings were removed. There were also improvements in Regular staff manning (henceforth the Training Major in each UOTC would always be a Regular) and greater priority would be given to ensuring all posts were filled with suitable candidates.

A further recommendation to improve efficiency was the grouping of UOTCs into Officer Training Regiments (OTR) and two pilot OTRs were formed as a trial in September 2011; Sheffield and Leeds UOTCs combined into Yorkshire OTR while Manchester & Salford and Liverpool UOTCs formed the North West OTR. These experiments were successful but there was resistance elsewhere, including Edinburgh where partnering with Glasgow & Strathclyde UOTC, while perfectly achievable, was felt likely to hamper some aspects of CEUOTC's performance and detract from the Officer Cadets' experience. The Glasgow MEC no doubt held similar views. The Honorary Colonel, Sir Malcolm Rifkind, felt sufficiently strongly about the issue that he chose to bring his considerable influence to bear:

I took a serious interest in the OTC Study that considered the possible merger of the Edinburgh OTC with that of Glasgow. I came to the conclusion that that would be a serious mistake and lobbied against it both in conversation with senior officers and in a letter I wrote.

The pilots reported to the Commandant RMAS in May 2013 and their conclusions, read against a background of plans to expand greatly the Reserve Army, were considered by the Army Command Group in September. Despite the potential for more savings from the formation of further OTRs, it was decided to maintain the existing structure of 15 UOTCs and two OTRs. This was presented, perfectly validly, as indicative of the value high command attached to the Units, but it is likely that they were influenced by the likes of Sir Malcolm and also realised that further OTRs would dilute the links to host universities, already tenuous in some cases, and seriously undermine one of the main roles of the OTC.

In the interim, with effect from January 2012, CEUOTC had rebranded itself as part of the 'Sandhurst Group' and introduced the new training syllabus. The Army Reserve Officer's commissioning course comprised five modules of which one, Module 4, would be delivered at RMAS and the remainder by UOTCs. Modules 1 and 2 broadly equated to the old MTQ1 and 2 and MLDP, as there was no change to the basic knowledge and skills required. Module 3, however, was new; a vigorous nine-day battle exercise for Officer Cadets who had applied for a commission and were intending to undertake Module 4, the three week commissioning course at Sandhurst. Module 5 was a post-commissioning course for new Reserve Officers, intended to introduce them to some of the practicalities of functioning in a Unit. Modules 3 and 5 were organised centrally with UOTCs alternating in running them for participants from several Units.

Curiously, this new role for Edinburgh UOTC, training non-University potential officers for the Army Reserve, was one that it last had, apart from some tentative experiments in the mid-1990s, in the first 17 months of the Great War – almost exactly 100 years earlier. It had turned full circle.

The planned expansion of the Army Reserve automatically created an urgent need for more officers, all of whom would be trained in large part by UOTCs. This led to a revitalisation of the Corps and a corresponding increase in establishment. CEUOTC was now authorised to have 200 Officer Cadets, including Potential Officers (POs) from local Reserve Army Units in addition to students of its host universities. However, as it was not straightforward to recruit the normal intake plus the additional numbers required in the September intake, the CO introduced a second intake in January 2014. This solved another problem: the Unit was

Sinclair Bothy, officially opened 1957 and demolished in 1991.
Forrest Anderson

Skottetoget, Norway, 1963.
Scott Lindsay

Skottetoget, Norway, 1963.
Scott Lindsay

Easter Attachment, Brig o' Don, 1965.
Diarmid Lindsay

Construction of
RE MACC bridge,
Helmsdale, 1986.

Forrest Anderson

The completed bridge, Helmsdale, 1986.

Forrest Anderson

Pipes and Drums, Folkstone, 2004.
CEUOTC

Summer camp, Gibraltar, 2014.
OCdt Eve Stott

The Officer Cadet
of 2014.

OCdt Eve Stott

Remembrance Day
Parade, Old College
Quadrangle,
November 2014.

OCdt Luke Craggs

Edinburgh University OTC/STC cap-badge 1908–48. Some contingents had a new STC badge but there is evidence that EUSTC retained the OTC badge.

Diarmid Lindsay

Edinburgh University Training Corps cap-badge, 1948–55.

Diarmid Lindsay

Left: Edinburgh Universities OTC cap-badge 1955–76.

Diarmid Lindsay

Below: Edinburgh & Heriot Watt Universities OTC cap-badge introduced in 1976. Retained since 1993 as the CEUOTC cap-badge.

George O. Sutherland

HRH The Duke of Edinburgh was appointed Honorary Colonel in 1953 and Royal Honorary Colonel in 2004.

not allowed to attest applicants until they were 18 years old but students from the Scottish education system could matriculate at 17. The January intake provided an opportunity for such younger students to avoid a twelve-month delay in joining and also gave the Unit a chance to make up any shortfall in the September intake and replace dropouts or medical failures.

Funding pressures also eased. Royal Salutes were resumed in 2013 and permission and funding obtained for the 2014 annual camp to be held in Gibraltar, the first overseas camp since 1990 and only the third ever.

On Saturday 24th May, over 130 Officers, Warrant Officers, NCOs and Officer Cadets flew out on an exercise that felt to the cadets like a real deployment. Their mission was to defend Gibraltar against terrorist insurgents disguised as economic migrants from North Africa and the Middle East.

Having settled in at Devil's Tower Camp, the home of the Royal Gibraltar Regiment, training started with early morning physical exercises and an initial phase of military skills improvement, including an introduction to fighting in built-up areas in a specially designed facility in the camp. The three platoons then had a week rotating between adventure training, leadership skills and a military exercise in the extensive tunnels, the latter widely viewed as the most exciting and popular event of the camp.

There was the usual busy programme of sporting and social events including the traditional Rock Run from the harbour to the highest point of the Rock, a formal 'parliamentary' debate covering topical military matters (such as Trident), a tour of the fortifications and a visit to the Royal navy base.

The culmination of the camp was the final exercise, an exhausting three days and nights trying to wrest control of the village from determined attackers. Heat, tiredness and the insurgents were not the only threats that confronted the cadets as Officer Cadet Churchhouse recorded:

The next day, my platoon was sent to recce the entrance to the tunnels, where a number of the enemy had been sighted. Before we could leave, the platoon was stopped by the TM, Major Walsh, who delivered the dire news that SUO Wu was in hospital after being savaged for biscuits by angry monkeys. In panic, we gratefully handed over our rations. It was only two hours later when Mr Wu swaggered unharmed into our rifle sights that we realised we had been conned and that, as a result, the staff were now eating our chocolate. If confronted, the TM will of course deny that this was his idea.

The end of camp was marked with a formal dinner at which the Guest of Honour was the Governor of Gibraltar.

Chapter 10

Reflections

THE OTC OF today would be recognisable to the cadets of 100 years ago but only just, since the changes far outnumber the similarities.

In 1914, before war broke out and changed everything, around 16% of all undergraduates were in the OTC; a fifth of the male students. They were unpaid, had the choice of serving in one of four separate Units (artillery, sappers, medics or infantry), and depending on their choice, might have to pay an annual fee for the privilege of doing so. There was virtually no social or military interaction between the Units. Cadets had standard army ranks and could be promoted to NCO positions while the officers all held Territorial Force commissions and were generally members of the University's staff. There was no Commanding Officer but there were a Regular Army Adjutant and NCO instructors and training focused on gaining Certificate B. The Units paraded several times each year at High School Yards, Bristo Square or Old College, often as part of a University event, and were inspected by the Principal and Vice-Chancellor, the Lord Provost or a very senior Army officer from Scottish Command, depending on the nature of the occasion.

Today, the cadets, one-third of whom are female, are all Officer Cadets and do the same infantry-based training. The officers are generally TA, though it would be pure chance if any were on the University staff. The Commanding Officer currently alternates between Regular and TA and the Training Major and NCO instructors are all Regular or ex-Regular Army. Cadets receive pay and can be appointed to Junior or Senior Under Officer posts.

They aspire to military qualifications but the emphasis is on personal development; adventure training such as overseas skiing, mountaineering and sailing expeditions are encouraged and facilitated. As in 1914, the training year culminates in a two-week annual camp.

The present Senior Under Officer, fourth year medical student Officer Cadet Olivia Atkinson describes her OTC career:

I first joined CEUOTC back in 2011 in my first year at Edinburgh University, mainly because I'd heard my sister talk about her own experiences in Tayforth UOTC so favorably [sic] and also because I was interested in pursuing a career in military medicine.

My first year was spent completing MLDP1, or what is now called MOD1 and passed in a blur of running up and down the Pentland hills, constructing bashas and learning the basics of a section attack. I caught the bug for OTC early on and relished the opportunity to spend my weekends doing something so different to my daily life at university. I'd come back on Sunday nights, having learnt how to operate an SA80 rifle (something I'd never have dreamed I would have even wanted to learn!), whilst my peers in halls would still be wandering around in their pajamas [sic]. I also made friendships with people whom I would never have met or spent time with otherwise and these friendships remain strong to this day.

During my second year, my year group and I had the daunting task of learning the combat estimate and how to successfully write and deliver a set of platoon orders as part of our MOD2. Over the New Year I went on Ex Northern Blade, the annual skiing trip to La Plagne where I gained my SF2 qualification after a week's tuition from military instructors. I also attended our Spring Camp during the Easter holidays up in Ballater, which provided a welcome distraction from the stress of pre-exam fever back in Edinburgh. There we spent time mountain biking, climbing and orienteering amid the beautiful Scottish scenery as well as participating in early morning Scottish Coun-

try Dancing – a surreal experience!

My third year was perhaps the busiest and most rewarding for me in the OTC. As a Junior Under Officer and acting section commander I was lucky enough to mentor ten first year cadets through their own MOD1. I also went on the ski trip again, this year to Les Deux Alps and worked on my SF3 qualification. I went on Ex Lightning Strike down in Blandford, home of the Royal Signals, and took part in an inter-OTC competition based around the work the Royal Signals do. This past summer I went to Gibraltar on the annual Summer Camp where we had a chance to practice FIBUA [Fighting in Built-up Areas] on our final exercise, go sailing as part of Adventure Training and learn more about being an officer in the British Army, as part of a two day 'officership package'. To top the summer off I then, with the rest of the drill cadre, took part in the changing of the guard at Edinburgh Castle, which is something very special that I will remember for a long time.

This year, in my final year of OTC, I was appointed Senior Under Officer, meaning I am responsible for, and provide support to all the cadets now in the CEUOTC and act as a link between the cadets and the staff. My time in the OTC has been at times challenging, incredibly varied, and almost always enjoyable. I don't regret for one second joining back in my first year.

While SUO Atkinson's experience has clear parallels to that described by 2/Lt Griselda Stevenson in 1986 and is broadly typical, certainly in terms of variety, of that of most post-WWII cadets, it is profoundly different from the purely military training of the early decades of the OTC.

An even greater contrast however, is in the relationship with the University. Instead of 16%, the proportion of Edinburgh's 62,000 undergraduates in the OTC is less than half of one per cent. With these coming from four separate institutions, the links between the OTC and the host institutions have inevitably been greatly weakened, but have not disappeared. The MEC provides a direct and secure link and, more visibly, the Unit parades each year in Old

College for Remembrance Day, when the Principals of the four Universities lay wreaths at the War Memorial. In addition, the annual Haldane Dinner is always well attended by senior academic and military representatives.

From the Army's perspective, the OTC as a whole is probably more highly valued now than at anytime in the past, even during the early days of WWI when its contribution was enormous and absolutely vital but not universally recognised or understood. With the current restructuring of the British Army and the proposed increased reliance on a greatly expanded Army Reserve there is a need for more Reserve officers whose training will, in large part, be the responsibility of the OTC. While this role is welcomed, it is not difficult to imagine a situation where a significant increase in the numbers of non-university Officer Cadets might reduce even further the places available to students, a situation that would not be welcomed by the host universities.

The value of the OTC to the Army includes intangibles such as instilling awareness in future 'leaders' of the Army's ethos, standards and culture. This is generally regarded as incapable of being measured. While that is correct, and while the futures of the current body of cadets cannot be predicted, the tiny sample of former cadets who have contributed to this history perhaps serves to provide an indication of the extent to which this objective is valid. They include a former Honorary Surgeon to the Queen in Scotland, a world famous author, a distinguished orthopaedic surgeon who commanded a TA RAMC Unit in Scotland and went on to be Honorary Colonel of Otago University OTC in New Zealand, an eminent biochemist and Director of a Medical Research Council facility in Canada and the first, and presumably later the most senior, female officer in the RAVC. Among other former cadets who have been mentioned to me are one who became an MP and Solicitor General of Scotland, many officers in all three armed services, including two Generals in the British Army, and a female medical student in the early 1960s whose family had no military background, but who was so inspired by the OTC that she chose to be the first female officer in the RAMC and rose to become the senior anaesthetist in the Army.

This impressive list of 'leaders' has come to light purely incidentally in the course of a mere few months research; if it is indicative of other periods then the OTC is reaching its target.

It is also possible to give a clear picture of former members' memories of their service. Several former Commanding Officers, Regular and TA, have talked of the pleasure and privilege of dealing with such an intelligent, pleasant and motivated group of young men and women.

For their part, former cadets almost unanimously feel that their experience was a highlight of that stage of their lives, definitely helped their personal development and, consequently, was a positive factor in their future career, whether within the forces or not. They frequently express admiration for their officers, the RSM (often described as a god-like figure and a magnificent example) and their instructors.

The officers, too, laud the NCO Permanent Staff Instructors; their contribution to the success of the OTC is immeasurable and must not be overlooked.

This history perhaps leads to an inevitable conclusion. Col Gibb was correct when he stated in 1988 that *the future of the Officer Corps lies in the University Officers Training Corps*. Given its additional role in the training of all officers for the expanding Army Reserve, this is perhaps even more true than Col Gibb envisaged.

The University Officers Training Corps is a national treasure of which CEUOTC is a proud and valuable element.

Notes to Chapters

Chapter 1

1   Lt Col Alastair Harwell, Commanding Officer of CEUOTC 2000–02, undertook extensive research on the history of the University Volunteers from 1859–1908 and this chapter draws heavily from his unpublished manuscript, although key elements have been independently verified and new material added.

2   In *The Queen's Edinburgh Rifle Volunteers*, the author states (p. 60) 'The University Company has no indifferent claim to seniority in the Brigade'.

3   *The History of Cambridge University OTC* by Hew Strachan, p. 123.

4   In 1908 the Battery Diary notes that they declined an invitation to become the 1st Battery by taking over 'the armament of the Left Half due to want of accommodation', suggesting it was the 'Right Half'. However, as the University Battery had been the junior of the two Batteries that had amalgamated, it would have become the 'Left Half' and this title is mentioned in Army Order 160 of 1908. The entry in the Battery Diary was an error.

5   Officers', Officers and Officer Training Corps are all commonly used. The apostrophe is more common in the early days and when Edinburgh OTC was given the title CEUOTC 'Officers' was used and I have standardised with that throughout.

Chapter 2

6   War Office letter dated 20th December 1909.

7   The matter of tartans is complex and contentious. The Glen Grant website states that a version of their tartan was adopted by the Black Watch and became the Government tartan. It also claims that other clans, including the Sutherlands, adopted the tartan but other, seemingly authoritative sources suggest that the Government tartan was originally Sutherland.

8   *Behind the Parapet*, the Journal of the Scottish branches of the Western Front Association, September 2013.

9   *Behind the Parapet*, September 2013.

10 *The Scotsman*, 5th January 1915.

11 Minutes of Senate meetings on 6th November 1913 and 14th January 1915, respectively.
12 *Raising and Training the New Armies* by Captain Basil Williams.
13 Minutes of Senate meeting, 30th March 1915.
14 Minutes of Senate meetings, 7th October 1915 and 23rd March 1916.
15 *The Student* newspaper.
16 *The Student* newspaper.
17 *The Scotsman*, February 1916.
18 *The Scotsman*, 11th December 1916.
19 *The Scotsman*, 22nd November 1918.

Chapter 3

20 Minutes of COMEC meeting ,18th March 1921.
21 *University of Edinburgh Journal*, Vol. 4, No. 3, p. 90.
22 *The Scotsman*, 9th July 1937.
23 *University of Edinburgh Journal*,1939–40, p. 137.

Chapter 4

24 *University of Edinburgh Journal*, 1940–42, p. 75.
25 *The Scotsman*, 1st May 1941.
26 *University of Edinburgh Journal*, 1940–42, p. 163.
27 Minutes of Senate meeting, 10th June 1942.

Chapter 5

28 *Daily Mail*, 30th December 1955.
29 Minutes of COMEC meeting, 9th December 1961.
30 War Office letter, Reference 3715, dated 19th November 1962.
31 *Town, Gown and Gun* by James B Duffus.

Chapter 7

32 Minutes of COMEC meeting, 23rd September 1966.
33 Minutes of COMEC meeting, 29th September 1967.
34 Minutes of COMEC meeting, 27th September 1968.
35 *The Times*, September 1974.

Appendices

PIPES AND DRUMS

The Pipe Band has been mentioned frequently in the text but merits a separate note.

Throughout its existence, the Band has been an important and highly visible element of the OTC. Before WWII it frequently paraded at major University events when it was also not unusual for the OTC to provide a Guard of Honour. Today, apart from the Universities' Annual Remembrance Day service, its activities are less University-oriented and more confined to the OTC, but they still make regular public appearances such as participating in the Royal Edinburgh Military Tattoo.

Members of the band have always had to be committed. Any military Unit takes pride in its musicians and Edinburgh's OTC is no exception. The pipers and drummers have always been expected to play well, march smartly and be neatly turned-out in their elaborate uniforms. All this requires practice and effort and, it will be remembered, is in addition to the demands of a degree course and their military training.

It was not always so. Piper Iain Maclaren told how in 1944–46, when the STC was winding down after the hectic war-years, he did no military training and former Pipe-Major Diarmid Lindsay gives a similar picture 20 years later:

Back in the 1960s there was a fair proportion of the band members who joined solely for piping or drumming reasons and there was always friction with the rest of the Unit when the band seemed to be privileged and perceived not to be doing the same hard work as the 'soldiers' in the Unit.

John Woodman (BCom 1963) gives a specific illustration:

In the summer of 1962 someone found out that the band had avoided the live-firing requirement for all OTC members for a number of years. Not used to receiving orders from high up, the order to present ourselves at Dreghorn Barracks surprised us but we dutifully attended in uniform. Given the allo-

cated number of rounds to be fired, we took our place on the range and fol-
lowed the discipline of target practice – except for one member who, as-
serting his independence from orders, fired off all his rounds in one go. He
was, of course, very quickly marched out of sight.

Such individualism was not welcome in a military Unit and happily was the exception: the majority of pipers and drummers did take the military training seriously
and many gained Certificate B.

However, the Band also played hard. A convenient illustration was their participation, no doubt in a private capacity, in the 1960s annual students' charities parades where it marched along Princes Street in a number of guises. One year,
dressed as clergymen, they styled themselves the 'Band of Hope'. The following
year they were in rags as the Highland Tinker's Band. On another occasion, wearing
homemade police hats and genuine police raincoats, borrowed by their coach who
was involved with the Police Pipe Band, they passed themselves off as that band.
Not surprisingly, this attracted the interest of the police but only fleetingly … after
the source of the raincoats was satisfactorily explained!

Today the number of applicants to join the OTC far exceeds the places available
and there is room only for individuals who will commit to the military leadership
training. Despite this, the Pipe Band is still able to attract sufficient Officer Cadets
willing to make the necessary extra effort and continues to flourish and play its full
part in the life of the Unit.

VICTORIA CROSS WINNERS

Five former members of the University of Edinburgh were awarded the Victoria
Cross during the WWI. Two of them were former members of the OTC.

LIEUTENANT D. L. MACINTYRE

David Macintyre served in the Infantry Unit before being commissioned into the Ar-
gyll and Sutherland Highlanders in May 1915. In 1916 he was seconded to the HLI
and was awarded the VC for actions near Arras in August 1918. The citation reads:

For most conspicuous bravery in attack when, acting as Adjutant of his bat-
talion, he was constantly in evidence in the firing line, and by his coolness
under most heavy shell and machine-gun fire inspired the confidence of all

ranks. Three days later he was in command of the firing line during an attack, and showed throughout most courageous and skilful leading in the face of heavy machine-gun fire. When barbed wire was encountered, he personally reconnoitred it before leading his men forward. On one occasion, when extra strong entanglements were reached, he organised and took forward a party of men and under heavy machine-gun fire supervised the making of gaps. Later when the latter part of our line was definitely held up, Lieut. Macintyre rallied a small party, pushed forward through the enemy barrage in pursuit of an enemy machine-gun detachment and ran them to earth in a 'pill-box' a short distance ahead, killing three and capturing an officer, ten other ranks and five machine-guns. In this redoubt he and his party raided three 'pill-boxes' and disposed of the occupants, thus enabling the battalion to capture the redoubt. When the battalion was ordered to take up a defensive position, Lieut. Macintyre, after he had been relieved of command of the firing line, reconnoitred the right flank which was exposed. When doing this, an enemy machine-gun opened fire close to him. Without any hesitation he rushed it single-handed, put the team to flight and brought in the gun. On returning to the redoubt he continued to show splendid spirit while supervising consolidation. The success of the advance was largely due to Lieut, Macintyre's fine leadership and initiative, and his gallantry and leading was an inspiring example to all.

The following month, Macintyre was wounded and returned to the UK. He recovered, resumed his studies and died in 1967.

LIEUTENANT S.T.D. WALLACE

Samuel Wallace served in the Infantry Unit of the OTC and was commissioned into the Royal Field Artillery in October 1914. He was awarded the VC for actions near Cambrai in November 1917. His citation reads:

For the most conspicuous bravery and devoted services in action in command of a section. When the personnel of the battery was reduced to five by the fire of artillery, machine-guns, infantry and aeroplanes, had lost its commander and five of the sergeants, and was surrounded by enemy infantry on the front flank, and finally in the rear, he maintained the fire of the guns by swinging the trails round close together, the men running and loading from gun to gun. He thereby not only covered other battery positions, but also materially assisted some small infantry detachments to maintain a position against great odds. He was in action for eight hours, firing the whole time, and inflicting serious casualties on the enemy. Then, owing to the exhausted state of his personnel, he withdrew when infantry support arrived, taking with him the essential gun-parts and all wounded men. His guns were eventually recovered.

Samuel Wallace survived the war, served in the RAF Volunteer Reserve in WWII and died in 1968.

UNIFORM NOTES

There are no comprehensive records of uniforms worn over the years and these notes are intended only as a general indication. For some periods there is scant information, sometimes merely a single photograph, and in such cases the source is indicated.

Lt Col Harwell researched the uniforms of the volunteers and the following four paragraphs are a summary of his findings.

When No.4 Company was formed in 1859, the uniform was a long, dark grey tunic edged in black braid, dark grey trousers, a dark grey cap with a black peak and a black, patent leather waist belt. Pouch belts of the same material were worn over the left shoulder, those of officers and sergeants being fitted with a chain and whistle. In 1863, the tunic was shortened with the braid replaced by black piping and a shako replaced the peaked cap. In 1875, the shako was replaced by a busby with black plume and chin chain and the pouch belts were discarded except for officers and sergeants. From 1878, a black Austrian Knot was worn on the cuffs as a symbol of 'volunteers'. In 1900, the busby was replaced by a drab, broad-rimmed slouch hat, of soft felt and two years later, the grey uniform was replaced by drab service dress with a light green Austrian Knot ('Drab' was the official term for the dull brownish colour that was to be the norm for army uniforms for many years.)

The Volunteer Medical Staff Corps wore a dark blue, high-necked tunic with black velvet facings on the collar and cuffs, dark blue trousers and a white leather waist belt. The helmet was dark blue with a small metal ball on a white spike. A white disc with a red-cross symbol was worn on the upper right arm.

When the Unit became the RAMC(V) it adopted the Regular Army uniform of dark blue with dull cherry facings and a silver Austrian Knot.

The Royal Artillery Volunteers' dress uniform was a dark blue single-breasted tunic with scarlet collar and Austrian Knot, dark blue trousers with a scarlet stripe down the outer seam, white leather belt and a black busby. A peakless forage cap was worn in undress uniform.

It is not clear when the Artillery and Medical Units changed to service dress but it was probably around 1903. Certainly by 1908 all three Units were wearing standard single-breasted, four-pocket, five-button tunic with a 'stand and fall' (or 'Prussian') collar, breeches and puttees. The Medical Unit wore the drab service cap (a plain cap in the style of a Glengarry) and white shoulder flashes with 'RAMC' and, underneath, 'Edinburgh OTC'. A white disc with a red-cross symbol was worn on each upper arm. Details for the Infantry and Artillery Units have not been established but are likely to have been parallel.

In 1913, the Infantry changed to kilts of the 'Glen Grant' tartan (believed to be Black Watch or very similar). The tunic was similar to the high-collared service dress but with cut-away skirts to accommodate the sporran which was dark horsehair with three white tassels and the OTC badge. The accoutrements were a brown leather belt with a rectangular single-pin buckle, a diced Glengarry with the OTC cap-badge, plain hose-tops and drab spats.

A 1914 photograph of an artillery gun team shows the cadets wearing peaked caps with the Royal Artillery cap-badge and brass EUOTC shoulder-titles. It is believed that only the Infantry wore the OTC cap-badge at that time.

Photographs from 1923 show several changes. The Infantry have adopted four-button tunics with open collars, shirts and ties. The Medical Unit still has the high collar service dress but wears a peaked cap with the OTC badge and RAMC collar badges. It is believed that there were no shoulder insignia.

Curiously, the memoirs of a 1924 Cadet recall that he opted for the Medical Unit because, unlike the Infantry he would not have to carry a rifle all the time and, unlike the Artillery or Engineers he would have the glamour of wearing the kilt. This is the only known reference to the Medical Unit being kilted.

By 1931, the Engineer Unit had also adopted the four-button open-collar tunic while the Medical and Artillery Units retained the five-button version. All three still wore breeches and puttees. The infantry still wore the Glengarry and OTC badge but the other Units wore peaked caps and the badge of their corps. Apart from the Artillery, which wore a dark leather belt, all Units wore a broad webbing belt.

In 1940, service dress was replaced by 1939-pattern battledress for all Units and it is believed that everyone wore the standard khaki Field Service Cap. Although there were Sub-units at least in 1944, one former cadet 1943–45 recalls that *'everyone was in the infantry and wore the OTC Badge. We all referred to the OTC and not the STC'*. Due to a shortage of shirt material, the BD tunic was worn on parade buttoned at the collar: off parade, the top button could be undone *'provided no civilian shirt or tie was visible underneath'*. In 1947 the Field service cap was replaced by the dark blue beret, for all except the Infantry.

In 1947 the Field service cap was replaced by the dark blue beret, for all except the Infantry.

It is believed that no shoulder titles were worn during the war but some time before 1962 were re-introduced with 'Edinburgh University' in an arc on the upper arm just below the shoulder seam and 'OTC' immediately below the centre. Both were blue on white.

In 1952, Number 1 Dress Uniforms were introduced. For the infantry it was the Black Watch kilt with a Piper Green doublet with blue slashes, the 7/9 Royal Scots Lowland bonnet with blackcock feathers and the 7/9 RS hose-tops. Other Sub-units wore the Number 1 Dress of their Corps.

Working dress was Battledress with Corps badges except for the infantry who wore the Black Watch Kilt and Tam o' Shanter with UTC cap-badge.

In 1953, a local innovation was the introduction of a badge to be worn by all cadets who had passed the War Office Selection Board (WOSB): white laurel leaves were worn at the top of each sleeve. It was felt desirable to create a distinction between cadets and assisted in training as the better qualified cadets were immediately recognisable.

After 'Officer Cadet' status was introduced in 1958, white cord or gorgette patches were worn on the collar or a white band on the epaulettes in shirt-sleeve order. The WRAC had a white band on their forage caps when wearing No. 2 Dress. Under Officers wore an Austrian Knot on each shoulder strap, that of the Senior Under Officer being more elaborate than the JUOs'.

In 1961, the CO felt that cadet numbers were such that it was possible to have a full parade, but the appearance would be improved if all men wore the same uniform instead of the distinctive uniforms of the different Sub-units. The 7/9 Royal Scots were about to cease wearing their kilts which were Hunting Stewart tartan as worn by the OTC Pipe Band, and WO approval was obtained for the kilts to be transferred to the OTC. Henceforth, dress for ceremonial occasions (and Skottetoget in 1963) was Battledress tunics with Hunting Stewart Kilts. As the WRAC had had to buy their Black Watch skirts, those continued to be worn.

In 1969, the Sub-units were removed and uniform standardised on the Infantry. Battledress was replaced by the green combat dress. Kilts and Number 2 Dress jackets were worn for ceremonial occasions.

As early as 1974, some Officer Cadets are seen wearing Disruptive Pattern Material (or DPM, a dark green and brown camouflage pattern) jackets but Combat dress continued in use for some years.

In 1978, the kilts were replaced by Hunting Stewart trews. Number 1 Dress was now trews with a Green Doublet and Number 2 Dress trews with a khaki Service dress tunic. The WRAC cadets' dress uniform was a box-pleated skirt of hunting Stewart tartan with a Lovat Green Tunic.

By around 1980, DPM working dress was in general issue and various versions of it continued as standard until 2012, when it was replaced by the lighter Multi-Terrain Pattern uniform developed in the light of experience in Iraq and Afghanistan. Number 1 and 2 dress remain the same. Brown combat boots were gradually introduced to replace the Combat Boot High introduced in the mid 1980s.

With effect from 1st September 2014, a Sandhurst Tactical Recognition Flash (TRF) replaced that of 51st Brigade, which the Unit had worn for several years.

PIPES AND DRUMS

When the Pipe Band was formed in 1909, it was authorised by the War Office to wear the MacFarlane tartan. There is no record of other details or changes over time but it is likely that it was an elaborate uniform in the style of the day and it might well be that it had changed little by the time former cadet Piper Iain Maclaren joined in 1944:

> I was kitted out with the OTC/STC pre-war pipe-band full dress uniform which was quite elaborate and significantly 'grander' than what was worn by Army bands at that time.
>
> It consisted of a MacFarlane tartan kilt and plaid, black leather waist and shoulder belts with imitation silver buckles, white horse-hair sporran with 'silver' mounted black tassels, white spats, red and black diced hose-tops, black Glengarry bonnet with black cock's feather, an ornamental dirk with Cairngorm stone and a black cloth tunic with 'silver' buttons and 'silver' braid. It really was quite impressive.

Three years later, the supply of MacFarlane tartan kilts dried up and the band obtained Hunting Stewart kilts from the Royal Scots.

The 1953 Clothing Regulations specify the band's uniform as:

Kilt: Hunting Stuart 8A
Tunic: Piper Green with dark blue slashes
Blue Glengarry with black cock feathers
Badges: Gold on Dark blue

Ten years later, the regulations altered the head-dress to a blue Glengarry with red toorie (RS Pattern) and rank badges to silver on blue; the kilt fastener was to be a glass-headed pin as for the Black Watch.

From around the late 1950s, the drummers wore a dark blue Tam o' Shanter but by the late 1970s had switched to Hunting Stewart trews and a dark blue Glengarry with dark blue, red and white dicing, still with the blackcock feather and the tunic changed from Piper Green to black.

CAP-BADGES

All badges are white metal. The original OTC badge in 1908 was the University of Edinburgh crest, a shield with saltire, an open book in the centre, a thistle above and a castle symbol below. A scroll underneath carried the words 'Edinburgh University O.T.C.' and the shield was surmounted by the King's Crown. The overall height was 46mm. This badge continued to be worn during WWII even though the

Unit was formally renamed STC. Although some universities introduced a new STC badge it is not clear whether Edinburgh did. In any case, it is known that at least some, and perhaps all cadets continued to wear the OTC badge.

A new, larger badge (69 mm high) was introduced in 1948 when the Unit became the UTC. This badge had the same crest as that of 1908 but the scroll read 'Edinburgh University Training Corps (TA)'.

In 1955 when the Unit reverted to OTC, the badge remained essentially the same apart from the scroll which now read 'Edinburgh University Officers Training Corps' and the crown became the Queen's Crown. The final change was the introduction in 1976 of the current badge, an open book, surmounted by the Queen's Crown against a background of a broad saltire. When worn on a khaki Tam o' Shanter the badge is backed by a patch of Hunting Stewart tartan.

Edinburgh & Heriot Watt Universities OTC cap-badge introduced in 1976.
George O. Sutherland

THE UNIVERSITY INFANTRY VOLUNTEERS

Date	Designation
27 June 1859[1] to 1866	No. 4 (University) Company, 1st City of Edinburgh Rifle Volunteer Corps
1866 to 1888	No. 4 (University) Company, The Queen's City of Edinburgh Rifle Volunteer Brigade
1888 to 1908	No. 4 (University) Company, Queen's Rifle Volunteer Brigade, The Royal Scots
July 1908	Infantry Unit of the Edinburgh University Contingent of the Senior Division of the Officers Training Corps

1 – This was the date of the first drill parade. The unit officially came into existence on 31st August 1859, the date its officers were commissioned.

Date	Officer Commanding
1859	Captain Alan Dalzell
1860	Captain Robert Christison
1877	Captain William Turner
1890	Captain Isaac Bayley Balfour
1897	Captain James Arthur Hope
1905	Captain Auckland Campbell Geddes

QERVB cap-badge, 1866.
George O. Sutherland

THE UNIVERSITY MEDICAL VOLUNTEERS

Date	Designation
November 1884	None. Unofficial volunteer stretcher-bearers
May 1886	Edinburgh Company, 2nd Division, Volunteer Medical Staff Corps
February 1902	Edinburgh Company, Royal Army Medical Corps (Volunteers)
July 1908	Medical Unit of the Edinburgh University Contingent of the Senior Division Officers' Training Corps

Date	Officer Commanding
1886	Surgeon Charles Walker Cathcart
1891	Surgeon (later Captain) David Hepburn
1903	Captain David Waterstone

THE UNIVERSITY ARTILLARY VOLUNTEERS ('THE BATTERY')

Date	Designation
January 1890	No. 2 Battery, 1st Edinburgh City Artillery Volunteers
February 1902	Left Half, 1st Heavy Battery, 1st Edinburgh (City) Royal Garrison Artillery (Volunteers)
July 1908	Artillery Unit of the Edinburgh University Contingent of the Senior Division of the Officers' Training Corps

Date	Officer Commanding
1890	Lieutenant (later Captain) James Cossar Ewart
1899	Captain Arthur Thomas Masterman
1903	Captain Francis Palliser Dods
1907	Lieutenant (later Captain) Reginald Clegg Gordon

CITY OF EDINBURGH UNIVERSITIES'

1859	No. 4 (University) Company, 1st City of Edinburgh Rifle Volunteer Corps
1866	No. 4 (University) Company, The Queen's City of Edinburgh Rifle Volunteer Brigade
1872	QCERVB occupied Forrest Hill Dill Hall
1884	Medical unit formed as unofficial volunteer stretcher-bearer Company
1886	Edinburgh Company, 2nd Division, Volunteer Medical Staff Corps
1888	No. 4 (University) Company, Queen's Rifle Volunteer Brigade, The Royal Scots
1890	No. 2 Battery, 1st Edinburgh City Artillery Volunteers, equipped with 16-pounder guns
1893	A Maxim machine-gun issued to No 4 Company. (First Machine-gun in Scotland)
1902	Edinburgh Company, Royal Army Medical Corps (Volunteers) Left Half, 1st Heavy Battery, 1st Edinburgh (City) Royal Garrison Artillery (Volunteers)
1903	Battery re-equipped with 4.7 inch QF guns.
1907	The Battery won the National Heavy Artillery Championship (The King's Cup)
1908	All three Units become Edinburgh OTC based at High School Yards
1909	Pipe Band established
1910	Artillery Unit converted to a Field Battery with six 18-pounder QF guns Engineer Unit established
1914	All equipment withdrawn. Only infantry training possible. Contingent became a full-time officer-training establishment
1919	Full-time training ends
1933	Marquess of Linlithgow appointed Honorary Colonel
1936	First Commanding Officer appointed
1938	Unit fired its first Royal Salute from Edinburgh Castle
1940	STC – Corps renamed Senior Training Corps as part of the Home Guard
1948	UTC – Corps renamed University Training Corps as part of the Territorial Army.
1950	WRAC Company formed as part of local TA Unit
1952	WRAC became a UTC Sub-unit
1953	HRH The Duke of Edinburgh appointed Honorary Colonel
1954	The CO, Lt Col A. W. Sinclair died on an exercise in the Cairngorms

OFFICERS TRAINING CORPS TIMELINE

1955	OTC – Corps renamed 'Officers Training Corps'
1957	Relocated to Forrest Road Drill Hall. Angus Sinclair Memorial Bothy (built by the OTC) officially opened.
1958	Cadets given status of 'Officer-Cadets'
1963	Skottetoget: Annual camp in Norway. WRAC Sub-unit disbanded.
1968	'The Edinburgh and Heriot-Watt Universities Contingent of the Officers Training Corps'
1969	Sub-units removed. Now three Wings: Basic, Advanced and Technical.
1972	Corps renamed University Officers Training Corps
1976	New EHWUOTC cap-badges issued
1978	Uniform changed from kilts to trews
1982	RA Sub-unit re-equipped with three 105mm Pack Howitzers
1984	New training syllabus introduced: MTQ1 and MTQ2
1989	Won Northern Lights Trophy for the third successive year.
1991	Sinclair Memorial Bothy demolished
1992	Light Guns replaced 105mm Pack Howitzers
1993	'City of Edinburgh Universities' Officers Training Corps'
1993	CEUOTC relocated to new Drill Hall at Colinton Road
1994	Drill Hall named Duke of Edinburgh House
1997	Won the King George VI Trophy. First Scottish OTC to do so.
2012	OTC became part of RMA Sandhurst. New modular training syllabus introduced

OFFICERS COMMANDING THE UNITS OF EDINBURGH

YEAR	ARTILLERY	ENGINEERS
1908	Lt R. G. Gordon	N/A (Formed 1910)
1909	Capt R. G. Gordon	N/A
1910	Capt H. Howden	Capt R. J. Inglis
1911	Capt H. Howden	Capt R. J. Inglis
1912	Major H. Howden	Capt R. J. Inglis
1913	Major H. Howden	Capt R. J. Inglis
1914	Maj J. E. Mackenzie	Capt R. J. Inglis
1915	Maj J. E. Mackenzie	Capt R. J. Inglis
1916	Maj J. E. Mackenzie	Capt R. J. Inglis
1917	Maj J. E. Mackenzie	Capt R. J. Inglis
1918	Maj J. E. Mackenzie	Capt R. J. Inglis
1919	Maj J. E. Mackenzie	Capt A. K. Paterson
1920	Maj J. E. Mackenzie	Capt A. K. Paterson
1921	Maj J. E. Mackenzie	Capt A. K. Paterson
1922	Capt J. A. S. Watson MC	Capt A. K. Paterson
1923	Capt J. A. S. Watson MC	Capt A. K. Paterson
1924	Capt J. A. S. Watson MC	Capt A. K. Paterson
1925	Capt J. A. S. Watson MC	Capt A. K. Paterson
1926	Capt F. E. Reynolds	Capt A. K. Paterson
1927	Capt F. E. Reynolds	Capt A. K. Paterson
1928	Capt F. E. Reynolds	Capt A. K. Paterson TD
1929	Maj J. B. Todd	Capt W. H. Mackenzie
1930	Maj J. B. Todd	Capt W. H. Mackenzie
1931	Maj J. B. Todd	Capt W. H. Mackenzie
1932	Maj J. B. Todd	Maj W. H. Mackenzie
1933	Maj J. B. Todd	Maj F. J. C. Moffat DSO
1934	Capt C. P. Beattie	Maj F. J. C. Moffat DSO
1935	Capt C. P. Beattie	Maj F. J. C. Moffat DSO

OFFICERS TRAINING CORPS 1908–35

INFANTRY	MEDICAL
Maj A. C. Geddes	Capt D. Waterston
Maj A. C. Geddes	Capt W. Darling
Capt A. S. Pringle	Capt W. Darling
Capt J. R. Bruce	Capt W. Darling
Capt J. R Bruce	Capt W. Darling
Capt J. R Bruce	Capt W. Darling
Capt J. R Bruce	Capt W. Darling
Lt R. Gentles	Capt T. D. Inch
Lt R. Gentles	Maj H. Littlejohn
Lt R. Kerr	Maj H. Littlejohn
Lt R. Kerr	Maj H. Littlejohn
Capt R. Gentles	Maj H. Littlejohn
Capt R. Gentles	Maj H. Littlejohn
Capt R. Gentles	Maj F. A. E Crew
Capt J. Ewing MC	Maj F. A. E Crew
Maj J. Ewing MC	Maj F. A. E Crew
Maj J. Ewing MC	Lt Col F. A. E Crew
Maj J. Ewing MC	Lt Col F. A. E Crew
Maj J. Ewing MC	Lt Col F. A. E Crew
Capt R. Kerr	Lt Col F. A. E Crew
Maj R. Kerr	Lt Col F. A. E Crew
Maj R. Kerr	Lt Col J. du P. Langrishe DSO
Maj R. Kerr	Lt Col J. du P. Langrishe DSO
Maj R. Kerr	Lt Col J. du P. Langrishe DSO
Maj R. Kerr	Lt Col J. du P. Langrishe DSO
Capt S. I. Russel	Lt Col J. du P. Langrishe DSO
Capt S. I. Russel	Lt Col J. du P. Langrishe DSO
Capt S. I. Russel	Lt Col J. du P. Langrishe DSO

On 28th May 1936, Lt Col F. J. C. Moffat was appointed the first Commanding Officer of Edinburgh University OTC
(Sources: *London Gazette*, Minutes of the Military Education Committee and of Senate)

COMMANDING OFFICERS

1936–45	Lt Col F. J. C. Moffat DSO
1945–53	Col A. D. B. Smith OBE TD
1953–54	Lt Col W. A. Sinclair OBE TD
1954–55	Major T. Little MC (2 I/C Acting CO)
1955–58	Lt Col D. I. H. Callender RS
1958–64	Lt Col C. S. Campbell MC TD RA (TA)
1964–67	Lt Col A. A. Shivas
1967–72	Lt Col C. H. K. Corsar TD
1972–74	Lt Col G. J. L. Coltart RE(V)
1974–77	Lt Col H. D. R. McKay
1977–78	Lt Col G. A. Thom RHF
1978–80	Lt Col D. J. Bayne RS (TAVR)
1980–83	Lt Col W. D. Cooper
1983–86	Lt Col J. W. H. Collins TD QOY
1986–89	Lt Col W. R. V. Percy TD
1989–92	Lt Col R.D. Abbot R Signals
1992–94	Lt Col R. Callander QOY
1994–97	Lt Col I. K. Hamilton RE (V)
1997–99	Lt Col S. W Crawford RTR
1999–00	Lt Col S. M. Bargeton BW
2000–02	Lt Col A. A. S. Harwell R Signals
2002–04	Lt Col E. Baxter QOY
2004–07	Lt Col J. H. T. Hancock SG
2007–09	Lt Col D. Urquhart RLC
2009–12	Lt Col D. J. Mackay RA
2012–14	Lt Col G. J. Mackenzie SCOTS
2014–15	A/Lt Col M. Hutchison QOY
2015–	Lt Col R. Connolly SCOTS

SECOND-IN-COMMANDS

1950–53	Major W. A. Sinclair OBE
1953–55	Major T. Little MC (Acting CO 1954–55)
1955–59	Major R. M. McKenzie MC A&SH
1960–63	No appointment
1963–65	Major D. A. Bullough RA (TA)
1965–66	No appointment
1966–75	Major G. S. Ferguson
1975–76	Major D. B. Marshall TD RSigs (TAVR)
1976–76	Major D. R. Douglas TD
1976–78	Major D. J. Bayne RS(TAVR)
1978–78	Major M. J. Stewart RE (TAVR)
1978–80	Major W. D. Cooper TD REME (TAVR)
1980–83	Major J. W. H. Collins QOY
1983	Major S. Hamilton
...	
1990–92	Major I. K. Hamilton RE(V)
...	
1997–99	Major S. Bargeton BW (V)
1999–01	No appointment
2001–02	Major K. Wilkinson RE (V)
2002–03	Major G. Ramsay KOSB
2003–04	Major W. Halliday RA(V)
2004–06	Major B. Shankland RSigs (V)
2006–07	Major F. Ward TD RA (V)
2008–09	Major C. Cowx Lancs (V)
2010–12	Major A. Williams TD SCOTS
2013–14	Major M. Hutchison QOY

TRAINING OFFICERS/TRAINING MAJORS

1949–51	Major A. R. G Pringle-Pattison QOCH
1951–53	Major E. J. C. Haigh HLI
1953–54	Major A. J. Rennie KOSB
1954–55	Major T. Little MC KOSB
1955–58	No appointment
1958–60	Major A. Reid RHF
1960–62	Major W. A. P. Wilkinson RHF
1962–64	Major I. A. Maclachlan RS
1964–66	Major R. C. Mothersill RS
1966–68	Major A. M. Warrack RS
1968–70	Major W. A. L. Rodger KOSB
1970–73	Major N. A. D. McCance RS
1973–76	Major C. F. R. Buchanan A&SH
1976–78	Major G. A. Thom RHF
1978–80	Major M. A. Villiers RH
1980–83	Major J. H. Nason QOH
1983–84	Major S. J. Lindsay BW
1984–86	Major A. M. Cumming GH
1986–87	Major P. H. L Frances
1987–89	Major D. D. de Chair
1989–92	No appointment
1992–94	Major W. E. Shaw RA
1994–96	Major P. Eydes KOSB
1996–97	Major S. Duncan-Smith
1998–00	Major D. Dobson RS
2000–02	No appointment
2002–05	Major D. Maitland-Makgill-Crichton HLDRS
2005–06	Major W. Halliday RA(V)
2006–08	Major D. Jack RS
2008–10	Major I. Pincombe RE
2010–10	Major A. Williams
2010–12	Major J. Stewart SCOTS
2012–	Major E. Walsh RE

ADJUTANTS

1908–13	Captain E. A. B. Clive
1913–14	Captain J. C. W. Connel KOSB
1914–18	Major J. E. Mackenzie
1918–23	Major C. Preston DSO
1923–27	Major W. Tod MC
1927–31	Captain M. P. Lothian
1931–34	Captain G. Murray MC
1935–35	Major G. Murray MC
1935–38	Captain C. A. R. McRae
1938–40	Major C. A. R. McRae
1940–40	Captain G. C. Williams
1940–41	Captain L. C. Gordon-Duff GH
1941–45	Captain W. H. Niven RS
1945–46	Captain D. A. P. Barry GH
1946–46	Captain H. McR. Gall Gray MC GH
1946–49	Captain J. McLean A&SH
1949–51	Captain W. G. R. Corkill RA
1951–55	Captain J. M. Hay RA
1955–56	Major A. L. Murray DG
1956–57	Captain H. M. Moore DSC KRIH
1957–59	Captain A. C. P. Pitcairn 13/18 H
1959–61	Captain W. A. Stockton GREYS
1961–62	Captain P. Woolcot RE
1962–65	Captain A. L. McMillan RASC
1965–68	Captain J. H. Nunn RE
1968–71	Captain H. G. H. Croft MBE RAOC
1971–74	Captain R. Adams RA
1974–75	Captain P. G. W. Smith RA
1975–78	Major (QM) P. McNaughton RSigs
1978–80	Major (QM) D. Cunningham RPC
1980–85	Captain E. T. Dorsett BEM
1985–88	Major B. Hill RGJ
1988–90	Major A. L. R. Prewer RA
1990–93	Major T. Buchanan RS
1993–01	Captain C. H. P. Inness RA
2001–10	Captain D. N. Lawson RLC(V)
2010–12	Captain G. Murray MBE RLC(V)
2012–14	Captain J. Murray AGC(SPS)
2014–	Captain D. Freeman RIFLES (Temporary appointment)

LOCATION OF UNIT SUMMER CAMPS

Year	Artillery	Engineers	Infantry	Medicinal
1908	Buddon	N/A*	Stobs	Aldershot
1909	Buddon	N/A*	Barry	Aldershot
1910	Barry	Buddon	Blair Atholl	Aldershot
1911	Barry	Buddon	Stobs	Aldershot
1912	Buddon	Ilkley	Ilkley	Ilkley
1913	Buddon	Barry		
1914	Stobs	Carlingnose	Stobs	Stobs
1915	Peebles	Peebles	Peebles	
1916	Barry	Barry	Barry	Aberdeen
1917	Barry	Barry	Barry	Aberdeen
1918	None	None	None	Aberdeen
1920	Buddon	Buddon	Buddon	Buddon
1921	Barry	Irvine	Gailes	Independent
1922	Salsbury	Stobs	Scarborough	Aldershot
1923	Redesdale	Ramsey Iom	Ramsey Iom	Ramsey Iom
1924	Larkhill	Brechin	Fleetwood	Fleetwood
1925	Buddon	Shorncliffe	Shorncliffe	Shorncliffe
1926	Stobs	Stobs	Stobs	Stobs
1927	Buddon	Blair Atholl	Blair Atholl	Blair Atholl
1928	Buddon	Scarborogh	Scarborough	Scarborough
1929	Barry	Catterick	Nairn	Nairn
1930	Buddon	Silloth	Silloth	Silloth
1931	Buddon	Catterick	Peebles	Peebles
1932	None	None	None	None
1933	Buddon	Stirling	Peebles	Peebles
1934	Redesdale	Callander	Callander	Callander
1935	Redesdale	Stirling	Nairn	Nairn
1936	Redesdale	Blair Atholl	Blair Atholl	Blair Atholl
1937	Catterick	Catterick	Catterick	Catterick
1938	Redesdale			

* Formed 1910

CONTINGENT CAMPS 1946–2014

Year	Location	Year	Location
1946	Dunbar	1981	Bellerby
1947	Dunbar	1982	Ripon
1948	Stobs	1983	Warcop
1949	Tain	1984	Beckingham
1950	Cultybraggan	1985	York
1951	Dallachy Airfield	1986	Warcop
1952	Fort George	1987	Westdown
1953	Buddon	1988	Inverness
1954	Findhorn	1989	York
1955	Findhorn	1990	Hohne, Germany
1956	Stobs	1991	Ripon
1957	Aviemore	1992	Crowborough
1958	Aviemore	1993	Nesscliffe
1959	Aviemore	1994	Beckingham
1960	Cultybraggan	1995	Sennybridge
1961	Cultybraggan	1996	Nesscliffe
1962	Spean Bridge	1997	Sennybridge
1963	Norway	1998	Barry Buddon
1964	Highlands	1999	Ripon/Catterick
1965	Gosport	2000	Sennybridge
1966	Drip/Cultybraggan	2001	Knook/Ypres
1967	Penhale	2002	Machrihanish
1968	Cultybraggan	2003	Ripon
1969	Benbecula	2004	Folkestone/Ypres
1970	Sussex	2005	Inverness
1971	Tilshead	2006	Ripon
1972	Aultbea	2007	Inverness
1973	Knook Camp, Salisbury	2008	Catterrick
1974	Benbecula	2009	Warcop
1975	Ripon	2010	Ballater
1976	Warcop	2011	Wyke Regis/Dartmoor
1977	Nesscliffe	2012	Kinloss
1978	Altcar	2013	Altcar
1979	Bellerby	2014	Gibraltar
1980	Folkestone		

Note: Until 1962, the WRAC contingent attended camp separately, usually at Guildford or **Liphook**

TROPHIES AND MEDALS

Ladies' Bugle. Presented To No. 4 Company, May 1860 by 'A NUMBER OF LADIES'

Ladies' Medal. 'to Be Shot For Annually 1860'

Challenge Medal 1884

Bayley Balfour Challenge Trophy

Recruit Medal 1891

Battery Challenge Shield 1893

Proficiency Medal 1894

Carbine Medal 1896

Monthly Carbine Competition 1896

Hope Quaigh *c.*1896

Corporals Cup 1902

Cossar Ewart Trophy 1907

Dods Cup 1907

Gunlayers Cup 1910

Signallers Cup 1911

The Somme Shell 2001 (A WWI 18-pounder shrapnel shell casing, presented by the author in 2001 to be used as an ad hoc trophy.)

Glossary

BAOR: British Army of the Rhine

CEUOTC: City of Edinburgh Universities' Officers Training Corps

CERVC: The City of Edinburgh Rifle Volunteer Corps

CO: Commanding Officer, in command of a major unit, here Edinburgh OTC

COMEC: Central Organisation of MECs. After 1962, Council of MECs

CMT: Certificate of Military Training

DTAC: Director [of] Territorial Army and Cadets

DVT&C: Director [of] Volunteers, Territorials and Cadets

ECAV: Edinburgh City Artillery Volunteers

ECRGA(V): Edinburgh (City) Royal Garrison Artillery (Volunteers)

EOTC: Edinburgh Officers Training Corps

E&HWUOTC: Edinburgh & Heriot Watt Universities OTC

GOC: General Officer Commanding

GOC-in-C: General Officer Commanding-in-Chief

MACC: Military Assistance to the Civilian Community

MEC: Military Education Committee

MOD: Ministry of Defence

MLDP: Military Leadership Development Programme

MTQ: Military Training Qualification

NCO: Non-Commissioned Officer

OC: Officer Commanding, in command of a Sub-unit.

OCB: Officer Cadet Battalion, a WWI officer training establishment.

OCTU: Officer Cadet Training Unit, a WWII officer training establishment.

OTR: Officer Cadet Regiment, a unit comprising two or more OTC units

PSI: Permanent Staff Instructor

RA: Royal Artillery

RAMC: Royal Army Medical Corps

RE: Royal Engineers

REME: Royal Electrical and Mechanical Engineers

RS: Royal Scots

R Sigs: Royal Signals

RSM: Regimental Sergeant Major, the senior NCO in a Unit

STC: Senior Training Corps

QERVB: The Queen's City of Edinburgh Rifle Volunteer Brigade

QM: Quartermaster

QRVB: Queen's Rifle Volunteer Brigade, The Royal Scots

TA: Territorial Army

TF: Territorial Force

UTC: University Training Corps

VMSC: Volunteer Medical Staff Corps

WO: War Office

WRAC: Women's Royal Army Corps

Bibliography

Books

Strachan, Hew (1976): *History of Cambridge University Officers Training Corps* (Tunbridge Wells: Midas Books).

Stephen, William (1881): *History of the Queen's City of Edinburgh Rifle Volunteer Brigade* (Edinburgh & London: William Blackwood and Sons).

Logan Turner, A (ed.) (1933): *History of the University of Edinburgh 1883–1933* (Edinburgh: Oliver & Boyd).

Williams, Capt. Basil (1917): *Raising and Training the New Armies* (London: Constable and Co.).

Mackenzie, Major John E. (ed.) (1921): *University of Edinburgh Roll of Honour 1914–1919* (Edinburgh & London: Oliver & Boyd).

Blair, J. S. G. (1982): *University of St Andrews OTC: A History* (Published on behalf of the University of St Andrews by the Scottish Academic Press).

Duffus, James B. (2012): *Town, Gown and Gun: A Centennial History of Aberdeen Universities Officers Training Corps 1912–2012* (James B. Duffus).

Minute books

Minutes of Edinburgh Universities' Joint Military Education Committee and associated reports and correspondence.

Minutes of COMEC AGMs.

Minutes of the Senate of the University of Edinburgh up to 1949.

Battery Diary and Minute Book (Edinburgh University Archives).

Journals and newspapers

Behind the Parapet, the Journal of the Scottish branches of the Western Front Association.

London Gazette

The Student, newspaper of University of Edinburgh's Student Association

University of Edinburgh Journal, various editions.

Other sources

Annotated photographs from the University of Edinburgh Archives.

Army Lists

UK newspaper archives (as referenced)